TRADING
UP

The Life-Maximizing Benefits
of Trading Temporal Values
for Eternal Treasures

PAUL DANIEL JOHNSON

TrustedBooks

BOOKS YOU CAN DEPEND ON

Sisters, OR

All Scripture references, unless otherwise noted, are taken from the New American Standard Bible, © Copyright 1960, 1962, 1963, 1968, 1971, 1972, 1973, 1975, 1977 by The Lockman Foundation. Used by permission.

Published by

TrustedBooks

a division of VMI Publishers
Sisters, Oregon
www.vmipublishers.com

13-digit ISBN: 978-1-933204-38-3
10-digit ISBN: 1-933204-38-9

Library of Congress Control Number: 2007923919

Printed in the United States of America

Cover design by Joe Bailen

Inquiries regarding speaking engagements, along with information about the author, can be obtained by visiting: www.pauldanieljohnson.net

Acknowledgments

Thank you to my wife, Wendi, who prays for me always.

Thank you to Joy Marple and Cecil Murphy,
for teaching and encouraging me.

Thank you to Dr. Fred Chay, whose passion is contagious!

Foreword

At a seminar in Tucson, I told the story of five-year-old Jennifer, who bought a $1.99 pearl necklace at the grocery store. She loved her necklace so much that she rarely took it off.

Jennifer's dad came into her room every evening to read to her and kiss her good-night. One night he asked her if she loved him. She answered, "Yes, daddy, you know I love you." He then asked her if she would give him her pearls. Astonished by his request because she treasured her pearls, Jennifer offered to give him her plastic white horse instead of her necklace. Her father kissed her cheek and lovingly said, "That's okay, sweetheart, I love you." A few nights later, Jennifer's dad asked her again if she loved him and requested her pearls. This time she responded by suggesting that he take her doll instead. As he kissed her cheek, he told her, "That's all right. I love you."

The next evening when Jennifer's dad walked into her room, she tearfully held out her hand and said, "Here, daddy; here are my pearls." As he took the pearls from her outstretched hand, he placed a lovely velvet box in her other hand. Jennifer opened the box and was surprised to see a beautiful string of pearls. Her father told her, "I was only waiting for you to let go of what is a temporary imitation so that I could give you what is genuine and eternal."

Paul Johnson's wife Jodee, who was losing her courageous battle with

5

cancer, attended this seminar and heard the anecdote. Since we were friends, she came up to me at the break and asked if I would share Jennifer's story at her funeral because she could identify with this young girl. Jodee felt that God was showing her how much He loved her by teaching her to let go of the temporal so she could live for the eternal reward. It was only a few months later that I had the privilege of sharing Jennifer's story at Jodee's memorial service.

It is a blessing for me to share the story again to introduce Paul's book about trading temporal satisfaction for eternal treasure. Paul has earned the right to share about this profound truth of "trading up". He is both candid and practical as he writes about the hard lessons he has learned regarding the value of living for eternity.

My prayer is that Paul's words will grip each one of us, so that when we are called before the Bema (Judgment) Seat, we will approach it with confidence because we have understood the eternal value of "trading up."

Cynthia Heald
Author of *Becoming a Woman of Excellence* and
Maybe God is Right After All

Contents

PROLOGUE
Scene at Bema 9

INTRODUCTION
The Mistake I Can't Make 13

CHAPTER ONE
When I *Trade Up*, I Can Live with a Purpose! 19

CHAPTER TWO
When I *Trade Up*, I Can Leave the Legacy
I Want to Leave! 27

CHAPTER THREE
When I *Trade Up*, I Can Maximize My Time! 39

CHAPTER FOUR
When I *Trade Up*, I Can Have Victory over Sin! 51

CHAPTER FIVE
When I *Trade Up*, I Can Experience a
New and Vital Christian Life! 79

CHAPTER SIX
When I *Trade Up*, I Can Be Free to
Love Others and Myself! 95

CHAPTER SEVEN
When I *Trade Up*, I Can Find Joy that Lasts! 111

CHAPTER EIGHT
When I *Trade Up*, I Can Reign with Christ! 131

EPILOGUE
Scene at Bema 173

A Note to the Unsure 175

Prologue

*"For we must all appear before the judgment seat of Christ,
that each may be recompensed for his deeds in the body
according to what he has done, whether good or bad."*

2 Corinthians 5:10

Electricity shot through my body, just like before a Midwestern thunderstorm unleashed its fury of lightning. The air was heavy and unmoving, making it difficult for me to breathe. Sand and pebbles scattered across a white marble-tile floor cut into my knees, but I hardly noticed. My body was numb, but my senses were sharpened and on edge. It felt just like the time I was taking a walk along a dark city street with its yellowed street lamps casting menacing shadows that were more like intruding enemies than soothing friends.

My eyes studied those around me. Most of them were on their knees like me, but some walked slowly forward around a corner into a room that was just beyond my line of sight. They looked like ordinary folks—tall and short, fat and skinny, old and young. That room, whatever it was, provided the only available light. I noticed a simple gold railing along white limestone walls that glistened within the near-total darkness, but no one was holding on to it. The walls themselves had the appearance of age but were perfectly cut, white, and reflected the light well. There seemed to be no ceiling in this place, nor sky and stars.

Fog hung in the air, partially obscuring large men who seemed to make up a security force, but they carried no weapons and were dressed in plain clothing. Even though there was something ghostly and mystical about them, their features were difficult to make out. They were in control: no words were exchanged, but they worked in an orderly fashion. They moved the line along with a deep sense of purpose.

What is this place? I screamed inside my mind. Minutes ago, I had been living my everyday real life. My fingers were flying across my computer keyboard as another software program took shape. Now I wondered what had happened to my work space. Where were my pictures, my baseball bobble-head dolls, my coffee-stained baseball cup and my prized green VIP parking sign that I had managed to garner from my last employer? *What is this place?*

The scenery reminded me of the museums I used to visit when I was a kid in grammar school. There was a sense of quietness or awe when I walked around inside those buildings. Every corner led to a room I'd just seen, and I often got lost. This place held that same kind of feeling. Perhaps "another world" was a good way to describe this very different, out-of-place scene that I hadn't experienced before. To be honest, I was more than a little frightened!

The line moved again, and I was close to turning the corner. The light arching around the bleach-like walls was pure and surprised me with its warmth. My mind drifted back to the many cold afternoons I spent watching baseball games in Minnesota. Every now and then the sun would peek out, and the welcome warmth would take the edge off a strong, north wind. It felt good, and so did this strange light which had a power all its own, just like the black fog that killed the Egyptian first-born in the old movie, *The Ten Commandments.* This light carried that kind of intangible power. You couldn't touch it, but you sure could feel it.

A vision flashed through my mind. I got up to move. My legs were working, but I'm not sure how. Locking eyes with a guard, I was startled for a moment by the depth of his richly-colored green eyes. (If you kept looking at him, you would find yourself whisked away to some whimsical place, unable to distinguish reality from fantasy.) I looked away, unable to hold his gaze. The line kept moving.

Finally, there it was! I had come around the corner, and it now stood directly in front of me. Its size was breathtaking. It was made of white limestone and trimmed in pure gold. Purple fabric—expensive as far as I could tell—was draped over the back of a large stone chair that sat on a sparkling platform. The oak tree-thick legs of the chair seemed sturdy and strong. Nothing could ever bring that chair down.

After catching my breath, I realized it wasn't the scene that caused me to fall to my knees again but the man sitting in the chair. This wasn't *just* a chair; it was a throne. The warm light I had felt was emanating from deep within this man's very being, the glow flowing through his skin. My mind was reeling. I felt the ground this time as my knees hit hard on the ground. This wasn't a place I belonged; it seemed like foreign territory. I was very scared!

I finally drew up the courage to look at him. He was pure white, with a robe that gleamed. His purity and absolute presence warmed me. The intensity of his love for me penetrated deep into my soul. I'd never felt anything like it, so I was speechless.

I looked into his strong and capable eyes that were also loving and kind. There was a hint of redness in them, as if there had been some tears recently shed. His hair was short, dark, and glossy. The chin on his strong and masculine face jutted out from defined cheekbones that would make an enemy flinch, but would make a friend feel safe. His olive complexion pulsing with beauty was the perfect filter for his inner light. I studied his strong arms and his calloused hands.

There was a dark hole in the palm of his left wrist. *No,* I silently pleaded. *This couldn't be. Is he the Lord? Is he the Messiah? Is this my judgment day? Am I ready for this?* Someday, I knew that this time would come. I'd done okay, I guessed. I tried hard, but still made mistakes. Now, I realized that none of my works could ever be good enough because I was in the presence of everything that was perfect. A new reality set in: I wasn't even close to perfect.

The Lord rose from His chair and asked me to stand. The world stopped. I was frozen in time. Trembling, I knew this was it; I would soon learn my fate. Would I hear "Well done, good and faithful servant?" He spoke…

The Mistake I Can't Make

The outcome for our fictional computer programmer is very much up in the air. The throne of Jesus reminded him that the treasures of the world weren't going to help him then: it was just between him and God. It was the *bema*, the Judgment Day for the Christian that each one of us will face. The consequences will be eternal.

Early one morning, with the cool desert breeze blowing through my hair, I drove toward a Tucson hospice. It was not unusual for me to be awakened by a call for help, but this night wasn't typical because I had planned to visit two patients in the same building.

As I entered the first room, I was warmly greeted by a group of family members gathered around a dying woman. They were believers in Jesus Christ, and their faith was clearly evidenced by their actions. As we talked, I learned something about the patient. A wonderful mother and grandmother, she had served Jesus during her life, so she was experiencing peace. As we prayed, I sensed a delightful joy that lingered over the room. This woman would soon be in the arms of Jesus. There was little doubt that she'd soon hear the words, "Well done, good and faithful servant" (Matthew 25:21).

I walked around the corner to visit my second patient of the evening but was frustrated to learn that the man had already passed away. I met his wife and a group of men in a visitor's room next door. The men were ministers of a church with unorthodox beliefs, and several of its leaders stood near the doorway. Unlike the atmosphere surrounding the first family, the mood here was cold, full of despair, and devoid of any joy. (I could even sense demonic spiritual beings in the room.) The widow showed no emotion as I reached out for her limp hand. The men didn't offer a handshake; they just wanted me to leave. I prayed with her and left immediately.

I had encountered two hospice experiences in the same building. Room number one offered a special joy and peace in the midst of death. After I left, they probably shared cherished memories of their loved one. The woman had received her reward at the feet of Jesus. Room number two, on the other hand, lacked any sense of hope or peace. The over-whelming atmosphere of darkness in the room was unmistakable. I wondered what the Lord had said to this man after he died. As I consid-ered the prospect, I shuddered with vicarious dread.

During this experience, God reminded me of the clear distinction between the bright future of believers and the hopeless destiny of those who don't believe. While those who don't know Christ constantly strug-gle to find a source of hope in their lives, Christians can experience joy amidst the worst hardships. The Lord promises peace in this life and rewards in the next.

How can we have lasting joy? What are these eternal rewards? Paul writes in First Corinthians about a time of judgment for believers which awaits all of us. "I laid a foundation, and another is building upon it. But let each man be careful how he builds upon it. For no man can lay a foundation other than the one which is laid, which is Jesus Christ. Now if any man builds on the foundation with gold, silver, precious stones, wood, hay, straw, each man's work will become evident; for the day will show it, because it is to be revealed with fire; and the fire itself will test the quality of each man's work. If any man's work which he has built upon it remains, he shall receive a reward. If any man's work is burned up, he shall suffer loss; but he himself shall be saved, yet so as through fire" (1 Corinthians 3:10b-15).

Many scholars believe that this particular event, spoken about in Revelation 20:6, will actually take place in heaven. This special time is usually referred to as the "believer's judgment," or the *bema,* the Greek word for "seat" or "chair," represented by the throne of Christ when we approach Him at that time.

Fortunately, salvation won't be an issue at the *bema.* Our place in heaven is already assured through Jesus' death on the cross for our sins. This will rather be a time when we'll receive rewards based on our service to Him during our lives.

The immense importance of the *bema* can be summed up by the following points:

- The Judge is Christ
- The object will be the believer
- The place will be heaven
- The mode of testing will be fire.

It's important for all of us to understand that eternal rewards are a tangible reality. Because we're saved through our relationship with Jesus (John 3:16; 14:6), we'll instantly be with Him in heaven when we die. The breadth of our experience in heaven, however, will be determined at the *bema.* It's here that the Lord will give us our rewards for a life of service. Those Christians who have been the most faithful will receive the greatest rewards.

I can catch a glimpse of what this might be like when I visit my local coffee shop. I can order a small cup or a larger cup, and they'll both be filled. They just won't contain the same amount of coffee. Although the small cup is filled to the brim, the person who purchases the large cup will enjoy more coffee.

In our final chapter, we will deal specifically with what type of rewards we can expect to receive at the *bema.* For our purposes now, it's important to understand that some will receive little, while others will receive more. All of us who go to heaven will be filled with joy and gladness, but the faithful Christian will drink from a much larger cup. Jesus explained this concept in the Sermon on the Mount. "Rejoice and be glad, for your reward in heaven is great, for in the same way they persecuted the prophets who were before you" (Matthew 5:12 NIV).

I struggle to live my life according to this promise. Everything on earth seems so appealing! I would rather take the easy road by desiring to avoid confrontation, limiting my personal sacrifice, and receiving admiration from people.

But it's in my quiet mediation time with God that I remember what's really important. I'm simply a servant who is not responsible to build God's kingdom. (God is perfectly capable of doing that without me.) I've not been placed here to build my own, however; I'm here to do whatever God wants me to do. If I decide to follow God's way, I'll receive a large cup of eternal rewards.

Kenneth Quick writes in his remarkable thesis, *Living for the Kingdom*: "The Holy Spirit acts as a down-payment of the inheritance, guaranteeing it to each believer in Christ. The Spirit also confirms the capability and responsibility of the child of God to draw upon His resources to live for God."[1] If I travel down the road of Christ, I'll also receive greater joy in this life. My relationship with Him will be intimate and loving because He'll always be drawing my soul toward Him. The wide, inviting roads of the world will fade into a distant memory when I only see and desire Christ.

The exciting thing about "trading up" is that not only will our eternal rewards be beyond our imagination, but our lives on earth will also be transformed. Jesus was clear about the precious nature of eternal treasures: "Again, the kingdom of heaven is like a merchant seeking fine pearls, and upon finding one pearl of great value, he went and sold all that he had, and bought it" (Matthew 13:45, 46). The Lord desires to give us His finest treasures because He loves us; however, He created us with a free will. We can decide to live for Christ; conversely, we can also choose to chase after the world's treasures.

In the first century, many people in the church at Colosse, an ancient city in Greece located forty-eight miles from Athens, made that choice. Some Christians had begun to pursue the world's treasures. Evil and greed were rampant, so the apostle Paul spoke out harshly against these foolish priorities. He wrote, "Set your mind on the things above, not on the things that are on earth" (Colossians 3:2).

Paul wrote this letter directly to believers during his lifetime, but that truth also applies to us. We can be saved and still lose precious rewards if we become "sons of disobedience" (Ephesians 2:2).

Roy Zuck and John Walvoord, in their *Bible Knowledge Commentary*, sum up what Paul is telling us in this passage: "Paul wrote, *set your minds on things above, not on earthly things.* That is, concentrate your concern on the eternal, not the temporal. 'Fix (your) eyes not on what is seen, but on what is unseen. For what is seen is temporary, but what is unseen is eternal.'"[2]

When we set our minds on heaven, we can "trade up." We can begin the process of putting aside natural desires of earthly comfort and satisfaction that frequently haunt us by simply making a choice. Soon, we'll discover that we can't hold onto selfish satisfaction and eternal treasure in the same hand. When we choose God's way, however, we will hear the words, *"my good and faithful servant!"*

---

1. Kenneth B. Quick, *Living for the Kingdom* (Doctoral Ministry Dissertation: Dallas Theological Seminary, 1989), 98.
2. J. F. Walvoord and R.B. Zuck, *The Bible Knowledge Commentary: An Exposition of the Scriptures* (Wheaton, Ill: Victor Books, 1983-c1985), 680.

1 When I *Trade Up* I Can Live with a Purpose!

I have to change that ring, I silently scolded myself as I staggered into the shower. It was 5 a.m. The hot water soothed my body, and my mind awakened. The day ahead was full, and the hectic schedule daunted me. It began with a breakfast appointment, followed by staff meetings, counseling sessions, hospital visits, and too little time to study for Sunday's sermon or even pray. The frustration of the day had already begun.

Trading temporal comfort for eternal treasure doesn't come easily for me. Lest you think that I have learned and daily practice this principle, think again. The scars from the ordeals of my own sexual abuse, along with the tragic death of my wife from cancer, continue to provide me with difficult hills to climb.

I often struggle with overcoming feelings of rejection aggravated by the abuse. All Christians have other issues to conquer, so we're all in the same boat. Although "trading up" is not easy to do, we believers share a common hope when we learn to depend on the power of the Holy Spirit.

For nearly a quarter of a century, I blamed others for my anger and lack of joy because of the emotional damage done in my life. I embraced temporal satisfaction by choosing to stay in my own protective comfort zone. Because I might have experienced psychological pain, I was afraid to allow myself to be healed. By making this choice, however, I threw away eternal rewards. I protected myself, even though the kingdom suffered in the meantime.

Not along ago, a friend helped me to understand how the consequences of abuse adversely affected my life and marriage. He frankly told me that my perpetual state of anger had helped me to survive over the years because it proved to me that I was still emotionally alive.

Because of my dysfunctional choices, a relational barrier that I built to protect myself stood between Wendi and me. After shutting down all of my vulnerable emotions, I descended into a dark abyss that only served to push her away. Unfortunately, I hadn't explored my wife; I had just exploited her. Despite my obvious love for Wendi, she'd gone many days without a word of affirmation. I had struggled to love her well, but my first impulse still was to run away. I had believed Satan's lie that told me I couldn't be loved.

I have lived a lonely life. Even today, it's difficult for me to have close friends, because my perception of others has been altered due to the scars of my abuse. Men with whom I work seem to exercise greater self-control and diligence than I, so even the relationships I have with them make me feel like an inadequate outsider.

While standing in the shower that morning, I sensed the gaping emotional hole in my soul and realized that I needed to deal with important issues. My fear of change, however, had been costly; it seemed easier for me to just numb the pain than to get well. Now, however, I knew that it was time for me to "trade up" to fulfill God's purpose for my life. John Piper writes that the pursuit of joy and God's glory are not mutually exclusive: "Oh, how passionately I agree that God created us for His glory! Yes! Yes! God is the most God-centered person in the universe. This is the heartbeat of everything I preach and write."[3]

If you were asked what the purpose of your life is, you might respond that it is to glorify God, which would be the correct answer. Jesus said, "Let your light shine before men in such a way that they may see your good works, and glorify your Father who is in heaven" (Matthew 5:16).

This is a great goal because joy comes when we glorify God. To fulfill the general purpose of glorifying God, we believers can pursue God and discover great joy.

This doesn't need to be an abstract, unattainable ideal because each of us can accomplish this goal in a different way. My individual purpose helps me to glorify God.

In order to discover my individual purpose, I need to possess the following:

- A vital and intimate walk with Christ
- A deep understanding of God's Word
- True Christian friends that will help me understand the truth about my strengths and weaknesses
- A lesser desire for comfort and satisfaction and a greater desire for eternal treasure.

An intimate walk with Christ will reveal both my spiritual strengths and weaknesses to me. A deep understanding of God's Word will keep me from striving for things that God never intended me to have. True Christian friends will help me see myself as I really am. "Trading up" means that I begin my journey of putting aside my own protective and destructive behaviors, replacing them with an intimate relationship with Jesus.

The greatest hindrance to Christian joy may be the pursuit of comfort. Many of us change churches because we're not comfortable with the type of music that is used for worship. Some of us stake out a certain pew, while others go a step further and ignore visitors. At any rate, staying in our comfort zones gives us control over our lives.

Yet, we don't *really* have control because we can't understand or contain God. To find and enjoy Him, we'll have to experience new people and places. Seeking comfort, on the other hand, kills our joy as Christians. The quest for comfort hinders our effort to "trade up."

All of us seek comfort in different ways. My individual comfort zone involves an area where vulnerability isn't allowed. I've learned to keep people close enough to have a relationship with them but far enough away so that I can't be hurt. My comfort zone revolves around this thought process: *Come closer, come closer. Stop!* The "come close, but don't hurt me" mentality has been one of the ways I embrace temporal comfort while forsaking eternal treasure. Because God is gracious, however, He awakened me before all was lost. He showed me that all I was pursuing in life was temporal comfort and satisfaction.

The pursuit of temporal satisfaction isn't always a mere quest for money, career, or other worldly activities that distract us from the goal of "trading up". The slavish devotion to *self* causes the greatest spiritual damage and loss of eternal treasure. Satan uses this stubborn selfishness to distract me from realizing my individual purpose in life. Blinded by this subtle deception, I then am unable to look for joy in the right places. Life instead becomes a self-centered quest for unattainable satisfaction.

I broadcast University of Arizona women's basketball games on a Tucson radio station. I've seen winning and losing players, as well as coaches, come and go. Winners win because they have placed their personal agendas aside and bonded together as teammates. They see the coach's plan, believe in it, and then execute it. Losers play for their own glory while ignoring the overall plan for victory. As Christians, our desire should be to please Jesus; however, our selfish commitment to comfort often makes it difficult to see our real purpose.

God's purpose for our lives can be disrupted by Satan, who wants to keep us in our comfort zone. He doesn't want us to trust God by stepping out and trying new things. If we abandon our commitment to comfort and focus on eternity, we can begin to "trade up" for better things. The apostle Peter warns us about our ravenous foe: "Be of sober spirit, be on the alert. Your adversary, the devil, prowls around like a roaring lion, seeking someone to devour" (1 Peter 5:8).

Satan wants to devour you by tempting you to get lost in the vain quest to make your life easy. Pursuing this path means that you'll miss out on many of the joyful experiences that God has planned for you. You can say no to Satan, however. By standing against the enemy, you clean the lenses in your glasses to see clearly. You'll then notice the things that matter for all eternity.

Each of us Christians will end up in the same place of judgment where every decision we have made will be examined. Jesus may address these kinds of issues:

- Why did you watch a football game while your wife waited to be romanced?
- Why did you sleep past your alarm? I waited for you to pursue our relationship.
- Your husband wasn't a perfect leader, but why didn't you trust *Me*?
- Why did the quest of raising perfect children become your highest goal?
- When did soccer practice become more important than church?
- Why did you sin to become popular?
- You could have served Me after you retired. Where were you?
- Why didn't you take time to memorize My Word?

These are the type of questions we may hear at the *bema*. We'll give an account to Jesus of how we lived our lives.

Eternal loss comes when we make decisions based on what's best for us in this world without a thought for eternity. John MacArthur writes, "Don't clutter your life with needless stuff...there are people who fill up—I call it people who fill up their life with trivia. It isn't evil; it's just insignificant. That's the encumbrance. It's like the illustration I used when I taught Hebrews...you can run the 100-yard-dash with an overcoat if you want, but you're not going to be very fast. And, when it comes to reward time, you're going to be at the rear end. Why not junk the overcoat and run?"[4]

—

Twenty-year-old Lenny was discouraged because he didn't have a career. The bank where he worked was a bore, and his personal life didn't show much promise either. He didn't have many friends and hadn't dated for almost two years. Lenny wondered if he could make his life better by finding out his purpose for living.

The people at church told him he could sing. He liked the church choir, but he couldn't attend practice on Wednesday because he was working extra hours at the bank to pay off credit card debt.

Drawing also was an enjoyable hobby for him. He thought about entering an art contest, but this idea seemed far-fetched to him. *Who'd want to look at my artwork?* he asked himself. Unfortunately, Lenny hadn't "traded up." His quest for temporal satisfaction instead took on these forms:

- His decision to ignore advice from people at his church
- His failure to cultivate long-term friendships
- His missed opportunity to enter an art contest because of his fear of rejection
- His debt that caused him to be trapped working a boring job at the bank.

Lenny's poor decisions had compromised his ability to "trade up," so his eternal rewards slipped away.

—

Sandra seethed. Because she arrived late for Sunday worship rehearsal, the music director replaced her with another woman. Sandra had so looked forward to this practice. Although the pastor often told her that she was one of the best singers in the church, a lesser singer had just taken her place. At the time, she wanted to get as far away as she could from church. *After all, how could God expect her to worship under these conditions?*

People in the church usually avoided Sandra. She was well-rehearsed and talented, but also highly critical of others. Because of her attitude, Sandra didn't have many friends, and she was very lonely. Life at home just didn't fulfill her, so she lived for every music rehearsal in order to do her best every Sunday. She loved to lead the congregation in worship. *Have I lost my touch?* she wondered. If today was any indication, the one activity that gave her joy was now in jeopardy.

Sandra was trapped in a quest to control her world, but in so doing, she'd forgotten how to pursue an intimate relationship with Jesus. Sandra's quest for temporal satisfaction took on these forms:

- Her attempt to glean personal worth from the church's music ministry

- Her use of leading worship to put her in the spotlight
- Her critical spirit that left her without friends.

Sandra had more to offer than she realized, but her desperate attempt to find joy in church music had deprived her of something greater. Because she was so busy with her various music activities, Sandra rarely had the time to get to know the Lord better.

Lenny and Sandra missed their individual purposes in life because of their slavish worship of self; subsequently, they threw away their irretrievable eternal rewards. Someday, Lenny's financial habits and fear will be addressed by Jesus at the *bema*. Sandra will have to give an account for her pride and critical comments. These believers have not "traded up" because they have refused to exchange temporal satisfaction for eternal treasure.

What about you? Have you found your purpose for living? You can begin to find your individual purpose by answering the following questions:

1. Is there an activity that gives me great joy?
2. What brings me positive feedback from others?
3. Is there an activity that is so enjoyable that I lose all track of time?
4. What part of me affects others in a positive way?
5. Have I asked God to help me?

Notes:

_____

_____

_____

_____

_____

_____

_____

A Prayer for Purpose:

Lord, thank You for choosing me to be a specific and important part of
Your kingdom. Please show me the individual purpose for my life. I submit to You. I ask You to do whatever it will take to make me the kind of
woman (man) that You created me to be. I offer You my life. I trust the
Holy Spirit to enable me to stand before Christ in confidence on the day
of the believer's judgment. Amen.

> *"For you were called for the very purpose
> that you might inherit a blessing."*
>
> 1 Peter 3:9b

3. John Piper, *The Dangerous Duty of Delight: The Glorified God and the
   Satisfied Soul* (Sisters, Ore.: Multnomah Press, 2001), 16.
4. John MacArthur Jr, "Bible Questions and Answers," a transcription from
   the tape, GC70-10, from a sermon delivered at Grace Community
   Church in Panorama City, California.. A copy of the tape can be obtained
   by writing Word of Grace, P.O. Box 4000, Panorama City, CA 91412 or
   by dialing toll free 1-800-55-GRACE. Copyright 1990 by John
   MacArthur Jr., All Rights Reserved.

2
When I *Trade Up* I Can Leave the Legacy that I Want to Leave!

This would be an emotional memorial service. In a few minutes, I'd be speaking to hundreds of mourners who knew and loved this seventeen-year-old boy. I also loved him, so getting through the service was going to be hard.

I was struck by the incredible range of people whom he'd touched. Packed into a small chapel were teenagers from my church, along with many friends and family members. I also noticed a group of teens that I wasn't prepared to deal with—the "punk rock" crowd, the kids dressed in black whose bodies are pierced with jewelry. These are the lost souls that go to raves in downtown Tucson. Desperately wanting to build a bridge of rapport, I tried to think of a way to reach them.

As is the case with any memorial service I've led, my notes were ready but I often didn't use them because I've found that I like to talk directly to the family. I seek to look them in the eyes and tell them about the eternal hope one possesses as a Christian. Today was no different. There was a problem, however; I had notes but nothing personal to add. I thought, *would these kids ever hear the gospel again? Would they set foot in a church again? This may be their one and only opportunity, and God is using a stodgy middle-aged man to fill the gap.* I prayed, *Lord, please show me what to do.*

I noticed a drum set that had been placed in the center aisle. A fine

27

musician, Timmy had used these drums to reach countless other musicians in Tucson with the gospel.

We were singing the final song before it was my turn to speak. Inscribed in large letters on the bass drum were the words "Celebrate Wounds," the name of Timmy's band. There it was! God had provided the bridge. *Thank you, Lord.* I strode to the pulpit with confidence and talked about this teenager's willingness to embrace the emotional pain caused by his suicidal depression from battling obesity. Each person in that auditorium had something in common: we were all wounded in some way or another.

To a very great extent, "celebrating wounds" was the legacy that Timmy had left for us. His willingness to face pain drew hundreds of unchurched individuals to him to hear the message of God's plan for salvation. I thank the Lord for Timmy's courage and use this story of "celebrating wounds" often. This young man had clearly "traded up."

What kind of legacy do you want to leave? Have you ever thought about that question? We all struggle with becoming tangled up in life's everyday pursuits. Even the famous existentialist philosopher Soren Kierkegaard saw the tedium and despair that comes when we focus on today and forget about tomorrow: "Boredom, for instance, is a warning that all the goods of life may turn to ashes in the mouth. When a man concentrates all his energies upon the pursuit of momentary pleasures, no matter how refined and subtle...his esthetic principles cannot rescue him."[6]

Kierkegaard wrote much about life's boredom. Most of his philosophy is based on the idea that we continue to want more things to fill our lives because we become bored with what we have. You may doubt that it's common to want more stuff. If you don't believe me, though, ask yourself when the last time was that you cleaned out your garage.

It's vital that we understand our individual purpose in life and strive to leave a lasting legacy. Empty striving for temporal satisfaction can be dealt with only when we consider what will be left behind. When we arrive at this place, we then understand that every action has a consequence. The consequences of our actions will affect many generations to come. This is how *purpose* and *legacy* fit together: when we discover our purpose, a lasting legacy will be set in place.

The Bible speaks about the importance of establishing proper priorities, which, in turn, lead to strong legacies. David, for example, was a
godly king; however, he paid dearly for his sin with Bathsheba. His kingdom was forever changed for the worse after he committed adultery and
murder. Even though his confession cleansed him from sin, he still lost
his first son, and his kingdom began to falter. These were the consequences of his sin.

There was also a cost related to David's poor parenting. In the book
of Second Samuel, we read about a rebellion fomented by David's son
Absalom, who declared himself king. David was forced to flee Jerusalem,
and the two armies collided in a deadly battle. A portion of David's
legacy had come back to haunt him.

Absalom's army marched against his father, but twenty thousand of
his soldiers were killed and many fled. Absalom attempted to escape on
a swift mule, but his long hair got caught in the branch of an oak tree.
When Joab, captain of David's army, found him suspended in mid-air,
he pierced him with three darts. Absalom's body was then taken down
and cast into a pit, where a heap of stones was later piled over his grave.

David cried out in this bitter lamentation: "O my son Absalom, my
son, my son Absalom, would God I had died for thee, O Absalom, my
son, my son" (2 Samuel 18:33 KJV). The great King David's failure to
train Absalom in the ways of the Lord had caused him incredible pain,
and he was left sobbing in regret. A number of valid questions must have
raced through his head after his son's death. *Would Absalom have been different if I'd paid more attention to him? Would any of this have taken place
if I'd stayed pure? Is the behavior of Absalom a consequence of my sin?* David's
legacy had been scarred by a series of grievous sin. Unfortunately, the
"man after God's own heart" didn't "trade up."

David's son, King Solomon, also disgraced the legacy of his father.
Even though the Hebrew monarchy attained its highest splendor during
the first half of his forty-year reign, the latter half was clouded by the
idolatries into which he fell.

As Solomon grew older, he married 1,000 idle women and lived
among them and their attendants in the palaces and pleasure houses that
he'd built. Still believing in the God of Israel, he didn't cease to offer

sacrifices in the temple or at the great feasts, but his heart wasn't right with God. His worship had become ritualistic and his soul was empty, so he sought any religious excitement he could find by building a pagan altar and worshipping idols. This was his vain attempt to "trade up." Displeased with his flagrant idolatry, God allowed Solomon's enemies to prevail against him. As a result, many judgments came upon the kingdom before his death.

Solomon defamed the name of his father. He had become a worthless son, who dismembered his kingdom and disgraced his name. God had blessed Solomon with great wisdom, along with royal heritage and favor, yet he settled for a destructive and ultimately unfulfilling lifestyle. Solomon didn't "trade up."

The Bible also records the stories of those who *did* "trade up." Joseph, whose integrity was the foundation for his rule in Egypt, restored his broken relationship with his brothers by forgiving them of their crime against him. Daniel stood against the idolatry and paganism of Babylonian kings, leaving behind a legacy of courage and strength. Ruth showed her faithfulness by staying with Naomi, her widowed mother-in-law, ensuring the continuation of God's messianic line. The apostle Paul left a legacy of discipline, faith, and hard work, and many lives were changed as a result. Peter was probably crucified upside-down in the Roman Forum for his steadfast devotion to Christ. These men and women understood that every choice they made in their lives shaped the legacy they would leave—long after they were gone.

Stephen Covey writes in his book, *Seven Habits of Highly Effective People*: "To begin with the end in mind means to start with a clear understanding of your destination. It means to know where you are going so that you can better understand where you are now, and to take steps that will move you in the right direction of your life."[7] Adopting this mindset allows us to "trade up."

Let me illustrate this concept by sharing my vision for my legacy. It begins in a small church where my funeral is being held. My family is sitting in the front row. The strength of this legacy will depend on how many of my family members know and love Jesus.

I can take steps to increase the likelihood of having many rows filled with Christians because of my legacy. First, I need to identify important priorities:

1) A profound intimacy with Christ is most important.
2) Accountability to other Christians is also vital.
3) A strong and vibrant marriage gives me emotional strength.
4) Prayer and Bible study will provide me with the courage to finish the race.

There's no easy way to finish this race. My relationship with Jesus is my only hope because my heart longs for intimacy that worldly pursuits just can't provide. This deep intimacy comes only through my submission to Him.

Submission has become a dirty word in our society. Some think submission means weakness, while others see it as a loss of personal control over one's life. The Lord, on the other hand, views submission as a key that unlocks intimacy with Him.

Because I want to sacrifice my life to God, I ask Him each day to make me submissive. I plead with God to do whatever He must do in order to make me godly. This prayer can be gut-wrenching because I offer my wife, children, career, and anything else to Him that might get in the way, but my surrender to Him leads to a deepening intimacy. God has answered this prayer by prying things and people I love away from me. Even though He has taken my first wife and changed my career, He replaced them by giving me more of Himself.

Accountability to other Christians helps me maintain my spiritual balance. I meet with a friend for lunch every Wednesday. We've been participating in this ritual for more than twelve years, and we know one another better than we know ourselves. In this honest relationship, we're free to encourage and confront each other, as well as share our private feelings in confidence. Our conversations center on biblical solutions to real problems. There are no "seven questions" or supposed formulas. This is real, man-to- man "iron sharpening iron." This kind of accountable relationship helps me to gain eternal rewards. Our meetings encourage me to do those deeds that will make my legacy last forever.

I am also accountable to my wife Wendi. She's welcome to ask questions about any area of my life. When I'm on the road, I tell her who I am with and why. More than anyone else, she can help me see blind spots that can lead to disaster. If I'm willing to listen to her, I can learn much about myself. Men, listen to your wives. Let them in your world. They're a God-given source of accountability and encouragement.

Moreover, my fellow pastors at Christ Community Church keep me accountable. Our staff has an "open door" policy. We're given the freedom to share our hearts and confront each other on important issues. The other pastors are allowed to storm into my office and tell me things that I often don't want to hear. I'm glad that they love me enough to confront me about issues. They don't always deliver the message in the right way, but that doesn't matter because they are usually right. If I shut them out of my life, I would take a major step backwards.

I understand that you may not have this type of accountability network in place in your life. You may think, that's great, Paul, but frankly, I have no one to talk to. I don't trust anyone, and I don't have the kind of personality that allows me to walk up to a stranger and ask him to be my mentor. So, I don't think I can do this. These circumstances in your life may be real, but believing that you can't establish an accountability relationship is not.

Paul wrote, "I can do all things through Him who strengthens me" (Philippians 4:13). The apostle doesn't say that I can do *some* things; he says I can do *all* things. You can form a meaningful, accountable relationship, but you need to first take the initiative.

To leave a lasting legacy, I must work to keep my marriage strong. Of all the goals I have mentioned so far, this may be the most difficult to achieve. As I've mentioned previously, I'm a victim of sexual abuse, which left me with a deep lack of trust toward others, including my own wife. Many times, I've shut Wendi out while I've tried to struggle through problems on my own. Because of faulty belief systems that I've developed over time, I have tended to see her as an enemy rather than as a friend. When I see her as a gift instead of as an adversary, however, I "trade up."

When I allow Wendi to see what I'm like inside, I become free to be myself. I'm also less vulnerable to sexual temptation and relational emptiness that can lead me astray. Wendi is a rock-solid foundation that God has given me to keep my emotional equilibrium.

My relationship with Wendi also gives me a chance to look beyond myself to see the needs of another and realize that there are more important people in the world besides just me. I "trade up" when Wendi becomes my most important earthly priority. A vital, strong marriage provides an opportunity to leave a lasting legacy.

I need courage to put all of this into place. We tend to define courage as "the willingness to suffer harm for the good of someone else," but this is an incomplete definition. To my mind, the most courageous people are the ones who remain strong in their faith. These are the ones who love their wives, model godly behavior to their children, and help build the kingdom until death. They are the real heroes. These men and women are not defined by how much money they've acquired or how many people they've influenced with their prestige, but rather by their faithfulness. Spiritual courage can be defined as "standing strong for Christ."

I 'm no longer impressed by the achievements of men, and the lives of celebrities aren't my primary concern anymore. I don't turn my head to admire the life of a CEO, but I'll sit for hours and learn from a courageous, faithful man.

Our church is blessed by a man named Stu Wilson, who has been a pastor for more than half a century. His faithful ministry has given him an immeasurable positive Christian influence on people, including thousands of patients and families in hospital rooms and countless teens who have enjoyed a long-standing, successful youth camp in Canada that he and his wife Jackie founded. This man has never wavered in his pursuit of biblical truth. When Stu talks, I listen. His rewards at the *bema* will be incredible, and I hope that I'll be able to watch the Lord honor him someday.

Men like Stu Wilson mirror the apostle Paul. They are single-minded, determined, and full of courage. Paul describes the focus of his life: "I press on toward the goal for the prize of the upward call of God in Christ Jesus" (Philippians 3:14). Like Paul, I will run my race for the eternal prize. Like Stu, I will pursue a lasting legacy, even though I realize this won't be an easy task.

This world is full of pitfalls. While I'm pursuing a lasting legacy, I need to watch out for obstacles. We can all identify with stones that cause us to stumble in our Christian lives. These "stumbling stones" can appear in the form of emotional affairs; a desire for material goods; an overriding desire for love and respect; anger; lust; selfishness; and a host of others. You would be wise to identify which ones are the most dangerous for you.

An inexperienced barge captain worries when he encounters fog because a river is full of dangerous obstacles. There are other vessels to avoid, bridges that can tear a boat apart, and numerous sandbars that can cause delays. Through proper charting, however, a seasoned captain can navigate past trouble. Likewise, the same principle can be true in our lives. We can identify obstacles, chart our course with the help of the Lord, and let Him navigate us to safety. For the riverboat captain, a reward awaits him at the mouth of the river where he will complete his business profitably. For the Christian, rewards await us at the *bema* when Christ will complete His business with us.

I've got plenty of stones of my own to avoid. My strongest earthly desire is for respect and admiration. God has continued to prune this area of my life, even though the process is painful. Although this sin is my responsibility, my past has created that particular area of weakness.

Because of the sexual abuse inflicted upon me, a part of me has been stolen away. Some have called this event "soul death." This is an accurate description of what takes place deep inside the heart of a sexual abuse victim: a terrible void has been created. My intellect tells me that only God can fill this place, but the message doesn't always reach my heart. I continue to struggle with the realization that there are no quick-fixes, but it's still hard to sit in pain and wait for God to fill me.

This healing process is obstructed when I try to escape. I can't "trade up," however, when I'm running away from God. It means that I'm moving toward the world's way: there is no middle ground. Jesus said, "He who is not with me is against me" (Matthew 12:30a). "Trading up" happens when I wait on God to fill my dark and empty soul.

I've described the struggles I face while striving to leave a lasting legacy. I'll battle with these issues in some shape or form for the rest of my life; however, I intend to run until the end. Nothing can stop me because Christ is running with me. *I can do anything through Him who strengthens me.*

—

Howard missed a putt that would have broken that elusive 80-shot mark while playing at his favorite country club. Yet, his frustration was reduced somewhat because he was headed to the clubhouse to enjoy some drinks with his buddies. Golfing had become a daily ritual for him. In fact, he wasn't sure what he'd do with himself if he didn't have his golf game to look forward to every day.

Howard had led a successful life. As a local bank manager, he directed his branch to become one of the most lucrative in the state. He worked many hours, but his family was well compensated for his time. His wife took care of her "dream house." His only daughter was close to completing her masters degree program at Brown University. Howard was also well-liked at his church. He was, of course, a big giver and often enjoyed the fact that his wallet gave him a little power when he needed it. He attended meetings regularly, and he and his wife attended a Bible study. Howard was indeed living the good life.

The golfing round was over, so the foursome headed to the clubhouse. When Howard's cell phone rang, he expected his wife to be on the other end because she often called to ask him when he'd be home for dinner. Instead, the caller ID indicated that it was his daughter's number, so he answered eagerly. It wasn't his daughter, however, but her shaken boyfriend. As Howard felt his legs go limp, he listened as the young man described a terrible car accident in which his only daughter had been killed, along with her unborn baby. She'd been drinking while driving. He hung up the phone, devastated by the earth-shattering news.

Howard had built a powerful worldly legacy, but he left a few important things out of the equation. Now, he'd have to deal with the fact that his daughter was gone. She was living with a boy he didn't know, and on top of that, she was pregnant. This last piece of information was new to him. Howard's material pursuits were catching up with him, and his worldly wealth now seemed hollow.

Howard's quest for temporal satisfaction took on these forms:

- His hours at the bank that took away time from his family
- His decision that church would be a place to be admired rather than a place to find Christ
- His obsession with golf
- His failure to lead his family toward having a deeper relationship with Jesus

We're not talking about a nasty man. Howard wasn't a wicked monster that repelled everyone who came in contact with him; he was just a nice guy who worked hard for the wrong things. He simply forgot that the world's treasures wouldn't last.

—

Sarah was tired of looking at the same walls and windows, and the television no longer held her interest. The social worker kept avoiding her questions about how long she would be here. *This rehab hospital is awful,* she thought. She loathed the place. The smells, the rituals, and the condescending nurses were beginning to drive her mad.

Worst of all, visitors were rare. Her pastor came by periodically, but she hadn't seen her son for months. *Some gratitude,* she thought. Sarah had provided inheritance money for him. When the purse was empty of cash, he disappeared. *Had she done the right thing?* "It's too late now," she whispered as she rolled over and tried to sleep.

Sarah's quest for temporal satisfaction took on these forms:

- Her use of money to keep her son close to her
- Her desperate attempt to find her purpose in life in her son and his family
- Her laziness: she didn't train up her boy in the spiritual things taught to her by her parents.
- Her failure to see the needs of people around her
- Her failure to understand that God still had a purpose for her

Like Sarah, many realize their mistakes after it's too late to change the consequences. Her tragic circumstances are played out in the lives of senior citizens around the world. Many wonder what they could have done to change their lives. This scenario can be avoided when they "trade up."

What about you? You can begin thinking about the legacy you wish to leave to the next generation by truthfully answering the following questions:

1. Do I know what I want my legacy to be?
2. What am I doing to create my legacy?
3. If I die today, what would someone say about me at my funeral?
4. Do I pray about my legacy?
5. Will there be anyone who went to heaven because of my life?

Notes:

_____

_____

_____

_____

_____

_____

_____

_____

_____

_____

_____

_____

_____

_____

A Prayer for My Legacy:

Dear Lord, I desperately want to leave a legacy that honors You. I don't want to look back and see a void that was created by poor choices. Please teach me what's important. Please show me what I can do to edify others, make new disciples, and teach truth to my family. Father, I want to leave a lasting legacy. Can You help me? I trust that You can. Amen.

"The conclusion, when all has been heard, is: fear God and keep His commandments, because this applies to every person."

Ecclesiastes 12:13
(from Solomon, the wisest man in the world, who forgot about his legacy)

5. Nichole Nordeman, *Legacy*, *"Live at the Door"*, compact disc, B000095J0J, ©2003 Sparrow Records.

6. James Collins, *The Existentialists, a Critical Study* (Chicago: Henry Regnery Company, 1952), 8.

7. Steven Covey, *The Seven Habits of Highly Effective People: Powerful Lessons in Personal Change* (New York: Simon & Schuster), 98.

3 When I *Trade Up* I Can Maximize My Time!

The two major currencies that drive our culture are time and money. Obviously, greed can make it difficult to "trade up." The less obvious stumbling block is the improper use of time. When time begins to control us, then our quest to "trade up" is in major trouble.

We Americans appear to be under the delusion that we're learning to better manage our time. Multi-dimensional cell-phones, on-line banking, website dating services, and drive-through churches *should* give us more time, but it just doesn't work that way. Something is very wrong.

If you're like me, you have less time than ever. *Where has the time gone?* I often ask myself. I can't imagine cooking every meal using a traditional oven and stove, or even relearning to write checks to pay bills. Although I should be the one in control of my time, the truth of the matter is that time controls me. If I can't learn to manage my time, however, I won't be able to "trade up."

When time controls us, we can't make proper decisions. For example, time spent "putting out fires" hinders me as I set goals, priorities, and boundaries for my life. When I am scurrying around solving problem after problem, my eyes aren't fixed on eternal things. I put too much time into trivial activities that will end up being burned to ashes at the *bema* anyway. How can I maximize my time? Let's find out.

Jesus is the perfect example of a man in control of His time. He is

God, but also fully human. Yet, he never panicked because He had a plan to take care of His spiritual needs. He knew His priorities and stuck to them. Let's look at how Jesus used His time.

1) *The Lord prayed often.*
Before Jesus walked on the Sea of Galilee, He spent time with God: "After He had sent the multitudes away, He went up on the mountain by Himself to pray; and when it was evening, He was there alone" (Matthew 14:23). A major event was about to happen, so it's no coincidence that He prayed. He was the busiest man who's ever lived, but He never failed to pray.

Jesus always prayed before important events in His ministry. He spoke with His Father before the "great confession" by Peter regarding His kingship, just prior to His earth-shaking Transfiguration. "And it came about that while He was praying alone, the disciples were with Him, and He questioned them, saying, "Who do the multitudes say that I am?" (Luke 9:18).

When something big was going to happen, where do we find Jesus? Do we find Him going over last-minute plans, worrying over details, or fretting over outcomes? No, we find Him on His knees, praying to the Father.

A few years ago, God gave me a wonderful opportunity to get a glimpse of the power of prayer. An elder at our church, Ron Kurth, was dying as a result of a malignant brain tumor. As the commanding general of the Tucson Air National Guard, Ron was no ordinary man. He was a powerful, godly person whom God allowed me to learn from during the last few weeks of his life. I'd often meet Ron at his home and read books to him, make his lunch, and do a few chores. During this time, Ron, reflecting on his life, told me about the things that were important to him. On one occasion, he looked at me seriously and said, "Paul, I want you to make me a promise as a part of my legacy." "Of course, anything," I said.

"Promise me that you will lead one man to Christ this year and disciple him."

"I will," I replied.

"Let me tell you one more thing," he said as he put his glass of milk down on the counter.

"Okay."

"If I could live my life all over again, I would do one thing differently. Instead of worrying about all of the details in life and staying busy with them, I would get down on my knees during every lunch hour and pray. If I had done that, I could have saved myself many troubles."

Later that week, Ron breathed his last breath. As I sat by his bedside, I thought about all I'd learned from him. I thanked the Lord for allowing me to view life from the perspective of a dying man. What more could I ask for? It was up to me now. I would honor Ron's legacy and "trade up."

2) *Jesus also knew the value of rest.*
Resting is a part of the wise use of time. Unfortunately, many of us find it difficult to take care of ourselves. Thankfully, the Lord set a better example for us. Even with His busy schedule, He rested, but never apologized or made excuses about it. Mark records this account: "And the apostles gathered together with Jesus; and they reported to Him all that they had done and taught. And He said to them, 'Come away by yourselves to a lonely place and rest a while.' (For there were many people coming and going, and they did not even have time to eat.) And they went away in the boat to a lonely place by themselves" (Mark 6:30-32). There must have been much to do, yet Jesus invited them to rest.

One of the most amazing examples of Jesus' willingness to rest is found in the Gospel accounts about the great storm that He calmed on the Sea of Galilee. Jesus rested so well that the disciples woke Him from a deep slumber in the middle of that storm. This story shows that the Lord was in complete control of His time. He prayed and rested in the midst of every circumstance.

3) *Jesus also spent valuable time ministering to individuals.*
We often think that only ministry to large groups is important. In fact, some pastors appear more concerned about numbers than individuals.

The first question I usually hear at a pastor's conference is, "How many people attend your church?" Maybe a better question would be, "How many people grow to be more like Jesus at your church?" This truly is a sad state of affairs.

The Lord, however, spent a great deal of time with individuals. Mary Magdalene, Zacchaeus, Nicodemus, and countless others were the recipients of Christ's ministry to the individual. In large crowds, He reached down to heal unknown people. He traveled through Samaria to meet with, of all people, an adulterous Samaritan woman. All of these encounters were planned and executed by Jesus, who always had a purpose for His time.

Sometimes after leaving the office at the end of the day, I say to myself, *I got nothing accomplished today.* When this happens, I've failed to realize that the most important accomplishments aren't always the most tangible. At times, Jesus' disciples believed that He was wasting time while doing eternal work. The woman at the well is a good example. The disciples didn't understand the eternal nature of what He was doing: "In the meanwhile the disciples were urging Him, saying, 'Rabbi, eat.' But He said to them, 'I have food to eat that you do not know about.' The disciples therefore were saying to one another, 'No one brought Him anything to eat, did he?' Jesus said to them, 'My food is to do the will of Him who sent Me, and to accomplish His work.' Do you not say, 'There are yet four months, and then comes the harvest? Behold, I say to you, lift up your eyes and look on the fields, that they are white for harvest. Already he who reaps is receiving wages and is gathering fruit for life eternal; that he who sows and he who reaps may rejoice together. For in this case the saying is true, 'One sows and another reaps.' I sent you to reap that for which you have not labored; others have labored, and you have entered into their labor'" (John 4:31-38). Only Jesus understood that His time was being used for eternal rewards. He was *receiving wages by gathering fruit for life eternal.* Jesus knew how to use time; He prayed, rested, and ministered to individuals.

Jesus used His time well, but we're tempted to waste it. Chuck Swindoll wrote these provocative words: "I'd like to play the Devil's advocate and tell you how to waste your time. Five proven ideas come imme-diately to mind. *First, worry a lot.* Start worrying early in the morning and intensify your anxiety as the day passes. *Second, make hard-and-fast predictions.* For example, one month before his July 1975 disappearance, Jimmy Hoffa announced, 'I don't need bodyguards.' *Third, fix your attention on getting rich.* You'll get a lot of innovative ideas from secular bookshelves (I counted fourteen books on the subject the last time I was in a bookstore), plus you'll fit right in with most of the hype pouring out of entrepreneurial seminars and high-pressure sales meetings. *Fourth, compare yourself to others.* Now, here's another real time-waster. If it's physical fitness you're into, comparing yourself to Arnold Schwarzenegger or Jane Fonda ought to keep you busy. *Fifth, lengthen your list of enemies.* If there's one thing above all others that will keep your wheels spinning, it's perfecting your skill at the Blame Game. Put these five sure-fire suggestions in motion and you will set new records in wast-ing valuable time."[8]

These five time-wasters are real and take us away from the things that matter the most. We spend our time spinning temporal plates on our fin-gers while the eternal ones are left unused. "Trading up" happens when we use our time for eternal purposes.

Don't get me wrong: there are temporal activities that also honor God. Housework, jobs, children's events, recreation, and learning are necessary parts of life. When we do them well, we glorify God. For example, 1 Timothy 5:8 tells us that one who doesn't make a living for his family is worse than a non-believer. Proverbs 31 honors a woman who takes care of her household. There are daily tasks that must be done that consume our time, but everything we do can be viewed in the light of eternity. A loss of eternal perspective, however, can cause us to get off-track. Then, we're tempted to waste time on activities that benefit no one.

I often get easily distracted by worrying about the condition of my yard, house, and my retirement account. When these things take top pri-ority in my life, I miss out on time swimming with my children, reading stories to my twins, and romancing my wife. Surprisingly, there are times when even watching a movie with my family has far more eternal value than a church activity.

At times, we must decide between "good" and "better." When we're submitted to Christ, we can make wise decisions about how we manage our time. Often, these choices can be very hard.

Jodee, my first wife, became sick with cancer. I was forced to make difficult decisions as the disease worsened, such as juggling work, taking care of the kids, and ministering to her. I think I did some things well, but I made some mistakes in the process. From this trying experience, I've learned that you always "trade up" when you spend time with your family. Family members come and go. Jodee died, and my children will leave home one day. This means that I only have a short time to make an impact on the people that I love.

When my kids were young, I thought I had forever to influence their lives. Now, I have a daughter in college. I wish I could retrieve a few years so that I could spend more time with my family and be less preoccupied with sports, work, and my own selfish pursuits.

During a recent men's seminar, I made a commitment to camp and fish with my sons, and I did. We left early in the morning and didn't catch a thing, but our time together was precious. Free to be ourselves, we laughed and talked about things that only men talk about.

Now, if my grass grows long, my pool gets dirty, and books need to be written, that's okay. There are more important things in life. Relationships and people are always more important than tasks and responsibilities. My children will be gone soon, so the other things can wait. I want to "trade up."

God gave me another chance with my second wife, Wendi, who brought a beautiful daughter and twin boys into my life. How I choose to spend time with them is my decision. But when I see Christ at the *bema*, I'll have to give an account to Him, because He'll ask me about the people under my care. Eternity tells me to use my time wisely.

The following is a list of steps I've taken to make better use of time. Some of these steps may appear trivial at first glance, but for me, they've made a huge difference in my life. They've helped me stay busy with eternal matters.

1) *I've learned to ask for help and delegate.*
Wendi pays the bills, and I have a wonderful administrative assistant at the church office. These people help me with everyday tasks that must be done. Others can help you as well. Ask your friends and family members to use their gifts to assist you. I've discovered that I "trade up" when I ask for help.

2) *I work with a "to do" list.*
This list currently consists of major items such as sermon preparations, writing deadlines, correspondence reminders, and other work-related tasks that need to be completed. I also place personal reminders on my list, including birthdays, gifts that need to be purchased for other occasions, and phone calls that must be made. After I complete a task, I simply draw a line across the paper and move on. This list helps me to focus on what's really important. I've found that I sleep much better because of my "to do" list.

3) *I have a large "dry-ink" calendar on the wall of my office.*
This calendar helps me to see months ahead. I can look forward to vacations, preaching dates, family functions, and various church events. Keeping this calendar up to date helps me to plan ahead. Unimportant events can be eliminated, while eternal activities are planned with care.

4) *I've learned to say no because I can't do everything.*
Saying no is an art form that took me a long time to learn how to do. For many years, I felt obligated to attend every function to which I was invited, but I've yet to lose a friend by saying no.

The failure to say no is a trap. Many think to themselves, *if I say no they may never again ask me to sing, play the piano, take part in the drama, coach the team, or receive a promotion.* We can trust God, however, with our future. He will bring these opportunities back around to us if they're His will.

My lack of faith was always exposed because I was afraid to say no. In his *Experiencing God* series, Henry T. Blackaby reminds us that what we do in a crisis will tell us how much faith we have.[9] I agree: to say no takes faith and courage. Learn to do this, and you'll be free from the bondage of trying to please everyone.

5) *I'm learning who I am in the Lord.*
I've learned about which spiritual gifts I have, so now my time can be directed more toward those specific areas. My gifts lie in the area of communication and pastoral care. When I accept this fact, I no longer have the desire to try everything and do everything: I simply want to communicate with others. Now realizing where to pour my professional energy, I spend time getting better in these areas while ridding myself of the desire to control and administrate. Some pastors want to stick their hands into every area of the church.

Obviously, my position comes with other duties as well. I love to make hospital visits and minister to people at funerals and weddings. Since I am most gifted in the area of communication, however, that's become my main focus.

To maximize our time, those who are gifted in administration can help us by administrating. Those who excel in other areas of ministry can help the church with their special gifts as well. Those to whom God has given the gift of evangelism, for example, can lead others to beginning a relationship with Jesus. Meanwhile, I will let God use me to speak and write His message. When we "trade up" by using our spiritual gifts, our time becomes a benefit rather than a burden.

—

Trudy checked her watch as she sped through a yellow light. If she got lucky and missed some traffic, she could make it on time to church. She tried to glance at the Sunday school lesson notes in her right hand. *Well,* she thought, *I hope God blesses this lesson. I certainly don't feel prepared to teach it.*

Trudy had a busy week at work. On Saturday, her sons played back-to-back soccer games, and then an evening barbecue eliminated her study time. When she got home, she was too tired to work on her lesson. Now, she would be late for church. She prayed that God would help her.

Trudy's quest for temporal satisfaction took on these forms:

- Her failure to study her lesson ahead of time
- Her willingness to settle for a lesson that could have been more beneficial for her students if she had prepared
- Her unwillingness to accept the responsibility of being a Sunday school teacher
- Her expectation that God would bail her out of a bad situation
- Her failure to make a better plan for Saturday.

Unfortunately, many of us are like Trudy because we don't plan ahead. Our church activities suffer from half-hearted preparation because we choose to waste time on other less important things. I wonder what God thinks of this kind of effort. Doesn't He deserve our best?

Many pastors and lay teachers are poorly prepared for their Sunday lessons, which just isn't fair to their listeners. This happens because of our busy lives and unexpected events that happen during the week, but we can still be prepared. When I walk into the pulpit on Sunday, teach on a Wednesday night, or broadcast a basketball game, God expects me to be prepared to give my best. I find it best to be thinking months ahead; this way, life's unexpected twists don't throw me. When I'm prepared and have planned well, the Holy Spirit changes lives.

—

My tears started flowing when my oldest daughter, Adina, walked onto the platform to receive her high school diploma. I knew that this day would come, just not so soon. My little girl in pigtails was all grown up. Where did the time go?

I looked around at the other families. They cheered and snapped photographs of their children. In a way, I was happy for them, but I was also jealous. I didn't have anyone with me to share the childhood memories of Adina. Wendi was there, holding my hand and doing her best, but I still felt alone. Sad memories flooded my mind. Adina's mother didn't live to see her daughter grow up, and this hurt a lot.

Adina has always been a special kid. "Spunky" is a great word to describe her outgoing personality. When she was in elementary school, she'd invite her friends to sleepovers and play Christian tapes—her goal being to share Jesus with her classmates. That's pretty cool stuff for a nine-year-old.

As I stood in the grandstand, I remembered so much. I recalled the plays that she used to put on, using our basketball court as a stage. We liked to swim together. I remembered reading to her, teaching her how to ride her bike, and taking her on special Valentine's Day dates. The time was now gone, and I couldn't get it back. There was an emptiness that could never be filled; Adina was moving on.

Now, I wanted more time with her. I would have paid a million dollars to take back each night that I rushed her to bed because I wanted to watch a game. Every morning that I slept in, rather than looking into her big eyes while eating breakfast with her, now seemed wasted. I wanted to relive the time we sat on the back porch and talked about camp. Selfishness had caused me to concentrate on my own needs while ignoring hers.

It took me a long time to grow up, and Adina had endured the brunt of my immaturity. Now, I wanted all of her childhood back as a "do-over", but the time was gone. It was floating away like a balloon without a string, and I could never catch it.

There would be no more snuggling together on a stormy night. She no longer needed me to lay out her clothes and get her dressed for church. Her dolls (the "little people") are packed away on the shelves, idle. (We played with the "little people" a lot.)

The opportunity to teach her about Jesus had flown by. I had only fished with her a couple of times. I too often failed to listen to her as a little girl, and now, here she was—an adult. Where had the time gone?

My quest for temporal satisfaction had taken on these forms:

- My decisions to put meaningless things like games and parties ahead of time with my daughter

- My choice to be weak: I didn't always speak into her life when she cried because I didn't know what to say
- My failure to encourage her
- My failure to tell her how much I loved her: it seems that I was always busy doing something else and rarely made time to sit and talk.
- My failure to do home Bible studies and teach her God's Word
- My failure to get to know her friends and understand and appreciate her life.

I hope you can learn from my experience with Adina. By God's grace, she loves Jesus, and our relationship has grown deeper. Regretfully, I'll never get her childhood back because it's gone forever.

Do you have children? Take the time to stare at them. Look deeply into their "morning eyes." Walk with them, tickle them, and make sure they know they're loved unconditionally. Don't let Satan convince you that they're an inconvenience. They may seem like they are sometimes, but God gave them to you for you to enjoy. The time will go by quickly. Don't let temporal satisfaction get in the way of the eternal treasure. I beg of you, please heed my words.

So, what about you? You can begin to maximize your time by answering the following questions:

1. Which of my activities have eternal value? Remember that exercise and rest are good things when done in balance.
2. Have I told anyone that I love them today?
3. Do I spend more time putting out fires than planning ahead?
4. Am I always late? Who do I hurt when I'm late?
5. Does God get the short or long end of my time?
6. Why do I procrastinate? Is it because I'm afraid to make a mistake?
7. Who owns my time?

Notes:

_____

_____

_____

_____

_____

_____

_____

A Prayer to Maximize my Time:

Lord, you have given me a short time on earth. Much of it has already slipped away. Please teach me to use every second for Your kingdom. Teach me balance. Show me when it's wise to rest and when it's wiser to work. Pull at my heart when my children need me. Help me to keep eternity in mind so that I can discern what's important. Use all of my time for Your glory. Amen.

> *"My son, do not forget my teaching, but let your heart*
> *keep my commandments; for length of days and years*
> *of life and peace they will add to you."*
>
> Proverbs 3:1, 2

---

8. Charles R. Swindoll, *The Tale of the Tardy Oxcart and 1,501 Other Stories* (Nashville TN: Word.:1998), 571-572.

9. Henry T. Blackaby and Claude V. King, *Experiencing God: Knowing and Doing the Will of God* (Nashville, TN: LifeWay Press, 1990-c2000), 120.

4 When I *Trade Up* I Can Have Victory Over Sin!

Here he was again tonight. It was late and his family was sleeping. His fingers were shaking, and he felt a pit in the middle of his stomach. Something inside, like a wave that came out of nowhere, was grabbing him so hard that he couldn't control it. Before he knew what hit him, he was swept away. Tim had been surfing the web for his favorite pornographic site, and he was both titillated and disgusted by it. Half of his brain told him to stop, while the other half told him that he needed this sensual stimulation.

Tim's life just didn't deliver the goods, and he was bored stiff. His position as an accountant left him unfulfilled. His kids didn't seem to need him anymore, and he and his wife never talked about anything important. He was dead inside; there wasn't any pain or joy in his life, only emptiness. He felt the need to live on the edge to know that he was alive.

Adrenaline flowed, and the beating of his heart quickened from the rush that came from this illicit behavior. This was the only time he truly felt like a man, which seemed to help him medicate his emotional pain. For a few moments, his life was like a thrill ride. It was dangerous, so that's why he did it. No relationship was necessary—just the quick fix of pornography. He knew the shame would come later, but the thrill seemed worth it at the time.

This behavior didn't fit Tim's concept of real Christianity; after all, he *was* a well-respected deacon in his church. It didn't matter, though, because he just had to have it. Without this secret excitement, he didn't have a life. He'd continue surfing pornographic sites, regardless of the cost.

At forty-three, Tim's life didn't look like he thought it should. The world didn't even know his name. He desperately wanted to accomplish something great, but the fantasy of the "American Dream" had faded away into the harsh reality of everyday living. He was left with nothing but a dreary life full of disappointment and average things. *Joe Average should be my new name,* he thought.

Tim's fingers kept moving over the keyboard. Every keystroke led him deeper and deeper into spiritual darkness. Each click on the mouse was creating a deeper hole for him, but he couldn't stop. He was being driven to destruction, and he knew it.

Surely, his wife knew something was wrong. During the past few months, their sexual relationship had deteriorated. Even though his attractive wife was still one of the prettiest girls he had ever known, he just wasn't interested. Having sex with his wife was difficult because he sensed that she held expectations for an intimate relationship. Terrified of intimacy, Tim didn't want that. After a sexual encounter with his wife, Tim would often feel deep shame because he fantasized about other women as he made love to her. Even though he knew how much he was hurting her, he couldn't make himself stop. A tawdry pornographic website was the only place that stirred any sexual feelings within him. Deep down in his heart, he hated this secret life. *Pathetic,* he thought. *I'm just pathetic.*

Tim had tried different ways to break his addiction. He prayed that the Lord would help him, sought counsel from a few close friends, and even attended a local group that specialized in sexual addiction, but nothing changed for him. Feeling hopeless, he'd accepted the fact that Internet pornography would be his downfall. He didn't think he could ever gain victory over that heinous sin.

There are many Christian men just like Tim who are addicted to pornography. Likewise, many Christian women pursue fake relationships in on-line chat rooms. Other believers struggle with alcohol and drug abuse, anger, out-of-control spending, overeating, and many other sins that steal the joy from their Christian lives. These addictive behaviors only create a deep emptiness inside the soul, leaving a person wondering if there's any hope of change.

One day, I was sitting in my weekly men's therapy group for victims of sexual abuse. It consisted of the usual group of guys whom I've grown to love and appreciate. Their perceptive insights have helped me to understand myself. On this particular day, the destruction of sin came to the forefront of the discussion.

One man shared that he'd committed a lewd act in public and now was feeling all of the shame that came with it. He was disappointed that he had acted out and feared that he might lose his job. This guy was literally shaking as he described what he'd done.

The group facilitator began to press him, trying to pinpoint a cause for his behavior. He asked him to describe his feelings before the event. The man said that he "lived on the edge to know he was alive." He mentioned that he'd awakened that morning with suicidal thoughts and wanted to *stop existing*. To deal with his overwhelming depression, he acted out sexually. Even this dangerous form of "medication" seemed better than living with deep, suffocating pain because nothing could be worse for him than that.

Unfortunately, medicating pain is not just for the unbeliever or sex addict. In America today, emotional pain isn't tolerated; there's now a pill for everything. Men in our society are taught that if they can't have an erection during sex, they can just take a pill rather than romance their wives. We can now swallow a pill for anxiety instead of dealing with its underlying issues. Had a bad day? Drink it away, gamble it away, vacation it away, but by all means don't deal with it or wallow in it. The American mantra is: "run from pain at all costs." After all, why feel pain if you don't have to?

Sadly, this is the wrong way to look at life. The astonishing, overriding reality for us as Christians is that God uses pain to bring us joy; this is a biblical principle that can't be challenged. The Bible talks in depth about painful trials that lead to new life. The apostle Peter wrote, "In this you greatly rejoice, even though now for a little while, if necessary, you have been distressed by various trials, that the proof of your faith, *being* more precious than gold which is perishable, even though tested by fire, may be found to result in praise and glory and honor at the revelation of Jesus Christ" (1 Peter 1:6, 7). This verse reminds us that failure to undergo the painful suffering of trials will deprive us of a refined and intimate faith that represents eternal treasure for us.

James tells us that new strength comes when we're willing to experience pain: "Consider it all joy, my brethren, when you encounter various trials, knowing that the testing of your faith produces endurance" (James 1:2, 3).

What a shame it would be if we stop short of the finish line. This can happen if we focus just on avoiding pain.

The apostle Paul even invited his "son in the faith" Timothy to suffer with him: "Therefore do not be ashamed of the testimony of our Lord, or of me His prisoner; but join with me in suffering for the gospel according to the power of God" (2 Timothy 1:8).

Christians in the early church had a fundamentally different view of pain and suffering from ours. Notice how the apostles reacted after they'd been flogged because of their faith: "So they went on their way from the presence of the Council, rejoicing that they had been considered worthy to suffer shame for His name" (Acts 5:41). Proud to suffer for the sake of the gospel, these men embraced pain. Joy was heaped upon them because they didn't run away. They "traded up" by boldly proclaiming the gospel, even though there was a heavy price to be paid. Undoubtedly, this also gave them renewed confidence and a steadfast assurance that God could take them through any troubled waters.

Much of our sin stems from a desperate attempt to avoid pain. Rather than embracing discomfort and meeting God there to get it resolved, we instead run to an earthly endeavor that provides immediate satisfaction. Tim drew immediate satisfaction from surfing the Internet. Others try to draw *life* from their children, spouses, favorite foods, and television shows. Whatever the medicine may be that works for any particular pain, Americans are quick to take it.

We're not so different from the Jews of ancient times. Just like us, these people sought to find rest in other things besides God. The Lord knew this behavior would only leave them empty inside: "But My people have changed their glory for that which does not profit. Be appalled, O heavens, at this, and shudder, be very desolate," declares the LORD. "For My people have committed two evils: They have forsaken Me, the fountain of living waters, to hew for themselves cisterns, broken cisterns that can hold no water" (Jeremiah 2:11b-13). The Israelites didn't live with an eternal perspective; they just wanted to avoid pain by consuming the world's medicine. It didn't work because the false water of the world became sand in their hands. They'd hewn a broken cistern. God stood by and watched. He was there, but they ignored.Him.

The human condition hasn't changed much over the past three thousand years. We're just as willing to make broken cisterns for ourselves, rather than patiently wait for the life-giving water of the Lord that springs up forever.

Having victory over sin can only come, however, when I live with an eternal perspective. I'd be easily deceived if I refused to consider the consequences of my actions. If I forget about rewards that are awaiting me, along with the account that I will give of my life to Christ at the *bema*, then I'm much more likely to seek after broken cisterns.

Just like Tim in the story at the beginning of the chapter, many people have fashioned broken cisterns out of Internet pornography, desperately seeking a thrilling remedy for pain in their lives. A recent *Crosswalk.com: the Magazine* article tells us that millions of Americans, including pastors, are hooked. According to Chuck Colson, who likened cybersex to spiritual crack cocaine, one out of five adults, approximately 40 million people, have visited a sexually oriented website. Of those who identified themselves as "born-again Christians," nearly 18 percent confessed to visiting such sites. Donna Rice Hughes, a leading anti-porn advocate, has cited statistics that indicate 39 percent of pastors currently struggle with internet pornography.[10] I consistently hear horror stories of fine young men gifted in the work of the Lord who have left the ministry because of their addiction to pornography.

Internet pornography doesn't just kill pastors; it sucks the life out of *all* those who visit its spider-like web. When a man or woman becomes hooked on pornography, marriages crumble, relationships with God are nearly destroyed, self-esteem crashes, and shame swoops in for the kill. Even though many types of sin incur similar damage, pornography is a graphic example of what takes place when we drink from broken cisterns. When we vainly attempt to find life from the world, we can't "trade up."

Why do believers in Jesus Christ, who should know better, become addicted to sinful behaviors? One answer could be the lack of eternal perspective and an intimate relationship with Christ. Dr. Morton C. Orman, the author of *The 14 Day Stress Cure,* says, "One thing that is true about most, but not all addictions, is they are often either the only or the strongest source of pleasure and satisfaction in a person's life. People who become addicted often do so because their lives are not fulfilling. They can't seem to find passion, enjoyment, adventure, or pleasure from life itself, so they have to invent these experiences in other ways. Whether such feelings come to them through gambling, getting 'high,' 'tuning out,' or becoming over-involved with the Internet, their work, their hobbies, or anything else, there is often a lack of other pleasures that drive people (at least in part) to crave pleasure from their addictive behaviors."[12]

The most telling sentence in this report from Dr. Orman's best-selling book is: People who become addicted often do so because their lives are not fulfilling. They can't seem to find passion, enjoyment, adventure, or pleasure from life itself. Some believers lack a sense of purpose and passion in their lives because they've given up on God and instead run to the nearest form of pleasure. Whatever gives us a sense of immediate life can take the place of God.

In Arizona we enjoy numerous small lakes. Having grown up in Minnesota, "the land of 10,000 lakes," I have finally learned to refer to Arizona's "ponds" as lakes. While many of these mountain streams and lakes offer wonderful fishing and boating, others don't.

When my family visits an inner-city lake, for example, I am always surprised to see fishermen on the shoreline. One look at the garbage strewn on the shore tells me that whatever fish comes out of that lake shouldn't be eaten. The point is this: at first glance, this lake looks like any other with plenty of water, as well as a shoreline. This appears to be a good place to fish; however, upon further investigation it's easy to see that there's something wrong here. The shoreline is unclean, the water is dirty, and the fish that come from its depths are probably not suitable for eating. This lake is not so wonderful after all and is definitely *not* a source of living waters. It may be inviting, but it's not fruitful; it is, in fact, a "broken cistern."

Now, let's take our fishing expedition elsewhere. Let's haul our gear and our courage to northern Arizona where a series of lakes in the White Mountains will offer us a chance to enjoy a day of sport. We find our lake, but things look much the same as they did back at our little lake in Tucson. There is water, a shoreline, and a number of people with lures in the water. Fish are being caught while boats are bobbing on the waves. Yet, a closer look reveals something different here. The fish that come from *this* lake are both edible and beautiful. The water is clear and the shoreline clean. This lake is not a *broken cistern,* but rather a source of pure and living water.

The lake in Tucson is much closer, easier to find, and offers a quick round of fishing, but the yield is foul and the ultimate effects disappointing. It's only when I'm willing to patiently drive for a couple of hours to find a better lake that I can find true enjoyment. The lake in Tucson is a fake, but the one in the White Mountains is real. Which would you choose?

Likewise, sin comes when we take the easy way out and choose the first lake. God is asking us instead to hold onto Him. It's only then that we can bask in the true and living water. Proud and rebellious, we ignore His plea and run for cotton candy rather than nutritious food. When the sugar high wears off, we limp back to Him, wondering why we continue to sin. The answer, although not an easy one, is to obtain an eternal mindset. To "trade up," we must forsake the filthy lake in Tucson and the cotton candy at the carnival. When we live with an eternal mindset, we become patient enough to wait for God, who's the true source of living water.

I recently stood on a balcony overlooking the Old City of Jerusalem and admired the breathtaking view. The Old City is located near what is now the walled portion of this holy place. King David probably stood in that very spot to oversee his kingdom. David reigned there before he purchased the threshing floor on Mount Moriah from Ornan the Jebusite. That very same threshing floor is now located on the Temple Mount where Christ will reign someday after He returns again.

It was from the balcony on which I now stood in the Old City that David may have noticed Bathsheba. The rooftops below me were nearby, so David wouldn't have had to look very hard to watch this beautiful woman. He had a perfect view of all that took place below him, and he *did* see her: "Then it happened in the spring, at the time when kings go out to battle, that David sent Joab and his servants with him and all Israel, and they destroyed the sons of Ammon and besieged Rabbah. But David stayed at Jerusalem. Now when evening came David arose from his bed and walked around on the roof of the king's house, and from the roof he saw a woman bathing; and the woman was very beautiful in appearance. So David sent and inquired about the woman. And one said, 'Is this not Bathsheba, the daughter of Eliam, the wife of Uriah the Hittite?' And David sent messengers and took her, and when she came to him, he lay with her; and when she had purified herself from her uncleanness, she returned to her house" (2 Samuel 11:1-4).

David was a godly man and a great king; however, his mistakes help us all to see our own vulnerabilities. He probably should've been with his troops in battle, since that's what kings usually did, but he chose to stay behind. It's possible that David was bored that evening because he had too much time on his hands.

We read of a man wandering around his palace who sees a beautiful woman bathing. David had a choice. Would he be patient and wait for God to fill whatever emptiness that existed in his soul, or would he yield to his lust which would only give him momentary satisfaction? Unfortunately, he chose the latter, and the consequences were disastrous. David got her pregnant and then killed her husband to cover it up. As part of the king's punishment, God killed the son born to him and Bathsheba. Moreover, David's kingdom became unsettled, and his own sons rebelled against him.

Was this tryst with Bathsheba worth the tragic consequences? Of course it wasn't. Impatient, David had chosen to sin, satisfying his lust while his heart remained empty. We better understand his pain by reading his heartfelt psalm of repentance: "Be gracious to me, O God, according to Thy lovingkindness; according to the greatness of Thy compassion blot out my transgressions. Wash me thoroughly from my iniquity and cleanse me from my sin. For I know my transgressions, and my sin is ever before me. Against Thee, Thee only, I have sinned and done what is evil in Thy sight, so that Thou art justified when Thou dost speak and blameless when Thou dost judge" (Psalms 51:1-4).

David traded precious eternal rewards for temporal satisfaction, an act that caused him immeasurable pain and suffering with the loss of two lives. Certainly, King David will gain many rewards in heaven at the *bema*, but some have been lost forever. During his lifetime, David had failed to "trade up."

My hypothesis is simple: when we live for the fleeting rewards of temporal satisfaction, we can't have any victory over sin. By living for eternity, however, sin can be defeated. Let me show you some practical ways with which you can begin to have victory over sin and "trade up."

1) *Identify your sin.* This is a difficult thing to do because it takes courage to look deep inside ourselves. What we find there may hurt, so it's easier not to look at all.

This part of the process is like turning on the light in an old attic. While the room was dark, no one was forced to deal with the junk strewn from corner to corner. When the light is turned on, the ugliness is clear to see. The room has to be cleaned, but this will take some hard work. (It felt better to live in ignorance.)

Even David had a difficult time identifying his sin because he rationalized his actions. When the prophet Nathan came to confront him, David didn't see himself as the sinner: "Then the LORD sent Nathan to David. And he came to him and said, 'There were two men in one city, the one rich and the other poor. The rich man had a great many flocks and herds. But the poor man had nothing except one little ewe lamb which he bought and nourished; and it grew up together with him and his children. It would eat of his bread and drink of his cup and lie in his bosom, and was like a daughter to him. Now a traveler came to the rich man, and he was unwilling to take from his own flock or his own herd, to prepare for the wayfarer who had come to him; rather he took the poor man's ewe lamb and prepared it for the man who had come to him.' Then David's anger burned greatly against the man, and he said to Nathan, "As the LORD lives, surely the man who has done this deserves to die. And he must make restitution for the lamb fourfold, because he did this thing and had no compassion." Nathan then said to David, "You are the man! Thus says the LORD God of Israel, 'It is I who anointed you king over Israel and it is I who delivered you from the hand of Saul. I also gave you your master's house and your master's wives into your care, and I gave you the house of Israel and Judah; and if that had been too little, I would have added to you many more things like these! Why have you despised the word of the LORD by doing evil in His sight? You have struck down Uriah the Hittite with the sword, have taken his wife to be your wife, and have killed him with the sword of the sons of Ammon. Now therefore, the sword shall never depart from your house, because you have despised Me and have taken the wife of Uriah the Hittite to be your wife'" (2 Samuel 12:1-10).

Notice the courage of Nathan. This prophet "traded up" when he approached the king with an admonishment from the Lord. Any king during that period would have possessed the power to take his life. Indeed, Nathan was a courageous man to tell David what he needed to hear.

Also note the judgmental spirit of David. He was ready to kill the rich man for taking the poor man's lamb, even though he himself was an adulterer and murderer. It's this kind of judgmental spirit that is clearly obvious when we refuse to see our own sin.

The point is this: although David had committed adultery and murder, he either couldn't see what he'd done or he'd rationalized it away. Either way, it was Nathan the prophet who made David aware of his sin.

David is not alone, for we all live in denial at some level. We don't want to see ourselves the way we really are; instead, we'd like to live our lives in a fantasy world. Then, we can pretend that we're better than everyone else so that we can be judgmental, maintain control, and never deal with pain.

When we're honest with ourselves by identifying sin in our lives, we'll experience pain because we can no longer believe the lie that we're better than others. This process can be uncomfortable and may cause tremendous psychological anxiety, but we mustn't be discouraged. This process of uncovering sin in our lives is well worth the time and effort.

I liken this process to me peering in the mirror each morning. I can tell myself all day and night that I look like Fabio; however, one look in the mirror dispels that notion altogether. That little twinge that comes when I see the raw, real image of me is just a glimpse of the pain that I can experience when I identify my sin.

Here are some practical ways that you can begin to identify sin in your life. First, *pray that God shows it to you.* The Holy Spirit is willing to help you see the sin in your life. Second, *ask other Christians to give you an honest appraisal.* This idea stinks at first. Who wants to have someone else rummage through your dirty laundry? The truth is, though, that others can see certain sinful areas in our lives that we can't see. Third, *ask God to give you a healthy, balanced view of your life.* Through this process, don't let Satan, the enemy, condemn you with the knowledge that you're a sinner. Remember that along with your sin comes the grace of God to both forgive and cleanse you. When you come to grips with this healthy view of yourself, you can experience victory over sin.

You may be thinking to yourself, *Paul, believe me, I have no trouble seeing the sin that has corrupted me and threatens to ruin my life. You have no idea how long I have struggled to overcome a particular sin. I'm just like Tim. My struggle may not be in the area of pornography, but I can certainly empathize with his plight.* If this is how you feel, join the crowd, but then move on with me to the next point.

After identifying your sin, it's time to come to grips with the nature and consequences of your sin. Let's be honest: sin is ugly and destructive, but it's your decision to do it. You're responsible for your sin; the devil *didn't* make you do it. You did it because you wanted to do it. You sinned because it temporarily satisfied a need in some area of your life, but all you did was create a broken cistern for yourself. James writes, "Let no one say when he is tempted, 'I am being tempted by God'; for God cannot be tempted by evil, and He Himself does not tempt anyone. But each one is tempted when he is carried away and enticed by his own lust. Then when lust has conceived, it gives birth to sin; and when sin is accomplished, it brings forth death" (James 1:13-15).

When all is said and done, the truth is still the truth. We all sit under the same umbrella of responsibility. When we sin, it's our choice; we're not victims.

It's easy to adopt a mindset that says, "My sin isn't as bad as your sin." In the Christian community, we tend to categorize non-believers into broad groups, labeling them as *the* gays, *the* liberals, *the* adulterers, and *the* sinners. Wait, I'm a sinner, too, desperately in need of a Savior. The only reason I'm saved is because of God's grace. I often thank the apostle Paul for reminding me of who I am without Jesus: "But God demonstrates His own love toward us, in that while we were yet sinners, Christ died for us. Much more then, having now been justified by His blood, we shall be saved from the wrath of God through Him" (Romans 5:8, 9).

Paul also reminds us that we can be content when we're intimate with Christ: "I know how to get along with humble means, and I also know how to live in prosperity; in any and every circumstance I have learned the secret of being filled and going hungry, both of having abundance and suffering need. I can do all things through Him who strengthens me" (Philippians 4:12, 13). Paul had discovered that the secret of contentment was pursuing a deep relationship with Christ. When he realized that only Jesus could fill the hole in his heart, he "traded up."

The apostle also understood that he was a terrible sinner. He never forgot that fact: "It is a trustworthy statement, deserving full acceptance, that Christ Jesus came into the world to save sinners, among whom I am foremost of all. And yet for this reason I found mercy, in order that in me as the foremost, Jesus Christ might demonstrate His perfect patience, as an example for those who would believe in Him for eternal life" (1 Timothy 1:15, 16). The truth is, as long as we rationalize, underestimate the effect of, or trivialize our sin, we will never gain victory over it. Accepting the fact that the nature of our sin is selfish and ugly is the only way we can "trade up."

By understanding the sinister nature of sin, we can grasp the consequences of our actions. It seems, however, that Christians rarely want to deal with the terrible results of sin. I realized that fact again this week as I counseled a man regarding his troubled marriage and the aftermath of a sexual affair. This man is now growing in incredible ways because, for the first time in his life, he is learning to rely on God. He is pursuing Him with a passion.

We got together on this particular morning to discuss advice that he'd received from another Christian. I was shocked when he told me that this man encouraged him to let his wife have her divorce so he could move on with his life. His reasoning was that "once she has her mind made up, it's over." I struggled with anger as I heard this ungodly advice. This type of counsel only allows people to avoid the consequences and lessen their emotional pain. To the secular counselor's mind, once the divorce was finalized, the psychological trauma would all go away, but that's just not true. Divorce is messy, and its disastrous effects last for a lifetime. The man who offered this piece of advice also missed the fact that my friend's relationship with the Lord was growing. Stopping the process now would only circumvent God's ultimate purpose for him. Sadly, his advice also failed to take into account the sovereign power of God; He can do whatever He pleases. God can certainly intervene and rebuild a marriage.

I told my friend to stand strong, even though he was experiencing intense pain at the time. My counsel was to stay still and let God speak to him in this difficult place. He wouldn't be able to run away from the consequences of his sin, but God could walk him through it. Holding onto God's hand would change him forever.

When we identify our sin and understand its consequences, we'll begin to understand its effects on us and on others. Then, we'll be less likely to "bow our knee" to the temptation and do it again. In so doing, we'll take a major step toward gaining victory over sin.

—

Now you are ready to understand that your sin is only temporarily filling a void. Use every means possible to discover where this hole in your life is.

When the pain of sin is striking you with full force, you should ask yourself why you did it. The answer to this question will help you identify the hole that is being filled by the destructive action.

As we look deep into our hearts, it's vital to remember that because of our sinful nature, we drift toward sin. Renowned theologian Anthony A. Hoekema writes, "The recognition that there is something wrong with the moral nature of man is found in all religions. In primitive religions, offerings, some of them even human sacrifices, are made to propitiate the gods for man's wrongdoing. The Koran, the sacred book of Islam, admits the universal sinfulness of man, understanding this sinfulness as being a violation of the will of a personal god. In Hinduism no personal god is recognized, and therefore sin is considered to be an illusion; yet the sacred books of Hinduism have much to say about sin, and prescribe many penances by which sin may be removed. Buddhism totally denies the existence of God; yet it affirms the universality of sin—for the Buddhist sin consists essentially of desire, either any desire or particularly selfish desire."[12] Hoekema also asserts that man's slant toward sinfulness is affirmed in literature and philosophy as well.

Psalm 51 confirms our bent toward sin, so we can't become complacent about it. We must be on a constant look-out for holes in our heart that are begging to be filled; then, we can ask the Lord to fill us. When He does, these gaps in our lives are eternally filled. The void in our life temporarily filled by worldly pleasure or defense mechanisms will quickly become erased. We must prevent the cycle of sin from starting over again by staying on our guard. When we allow ourselves to get complacent and become vulnerable, Satan attacks and we let our guard down. We can't "trade up" when we are trapped in this cycle.

A boat without an anchor will drift. A fishing lure will succumb to a current. A swimmer floating aimlessly in the water will quietly move with the waves. Likewise, a complacent Christian without an anchored spiritual life will drift away from God, which will affect his spiritual standing both in this life and for eternity. To fight complacency, become pro-active in your Christian walk and move toward God. If you do nothing, you'll just drift away from Him.

Remember the computer programmer whom we met in the very first pages of this book? He's now at the point of seeing the fruit that has come from his life. He either will, or will not, receive rewards at the *bema*. We'll all be there someday, looking straight into the eyes of Jesus and having to give an account for our lives.

It's time that we understood more about ourselves by examining the sins with which we consistently struggle. Then, we can identify which *broken cistern* we use to fill our emptiness.

Practical steps can be taken to move toward this goal. But be forewarned: herein lies a great adventure that will drive us to the very cores of our souls. This trip isn't for the faint-hearted because we're now going deeper than most Christians ever go. Nevertheless, it's only by going on this journey that we can find the holes in our lives, as well as God's heart for us.

First, in order to find the places in which our emptiness dwells—the ones that are filled by broken cisterns—*we must consider our past.* Although we don't want to dwell there, understanding our past can be extremely helpful. Questions such as, "What were my parents really like?"; "How did that sexual experience during college change my view about me and men or women in general?"; "In what ways did divorce shatter my soul?"; "How was I affected when my teacher told me that I wasn't going to be as good as everyone else?"; and "How does the truth differ from imagination?" can help us unlock patterns of behavior that have been buried for years. An honest, soul-searching examination of the past can help us understand the defense mechanisms that we've put in place to avoid pain. When we've experienced traumatic events, we just don't want to be hurt again.

Second, we can examine how our past hurts shape our *current reality.* It's amazing how an event that happened years ago can still affect our lives. For example, as a young boy, I was playing with a friend in a park near my home. The boy's father drove up in his pick-up truck and told his son to get in. I assumed that he was talking to both of us, so I hopped in the back as he was driving away. The man turned back to me and screamed, "What are you doing there?" I jumped off and pretended that nothing was wrong. To this day, I can still feel the pain of that moment in my heart; that event still affects me. When someone doesn't include me, I experience that same feeling of rejection. I often feel a deep need to be the center of the universe; however, I can only satisfy this longing by asking Jesus to fill the void of rejection. He can and will do this, but it's my choice to ask Him.

What's your "big hurt"? God can unlock incredible doors if you're willing to explore your heart. I have others like the one I've described above, such as the emotional pain from being sexually abused. In my current reality, this has resulted in a lingering belief that I can't trust myself. It's also brought shame that tells me I'm not worthy to be loved by God or anyone else. I've deadened myself to avoid further pain. Even though broken cisterns are always available, developing an intimate relationship with Christ is the only choice that will give me victory over sin. His deep, abiding love alone will fill all my empty spaces.

Take a moment and list painful experiences from your past. These events are probably affecting your struggle against sin. Pray that God will open your heart because it's time to be honest. Tears are welcome.

Notes:

_____

_____

_____

_____

_____

_____

_____

How do you feel now? It's time to take action. God has given you an opportunity to embrace the healing hand of Jesus, so don't let it slip away. Seek the help of friends, a Christian counselor, or your pastor. Begin to understand your wounds. You have probably already discovered many ways to make your pain go away, but they may not be healthy. Remember that sinning can only temporarily medicate the pain.

In order to experience true victory over sin, we need to directly confront it; then, we can clearly see its selfishness and ugliness. By exploring the holes in our souls that cause us to run to those sinful, empty fountains of the world, we now have more information that equips us to fight. To fight well, we must learn more about the demonic forces that are bent on destroying us. Fortunately, there are also spiritual forces that heal us.

In order to take the next step and have victory over sin, we must *learn more about the enemy.* I don't want us to dwell on Satan, but it's helpful to understand the methods he uses in his attempts to discourage and destroy us.

Satan is a real being created by God. The prophet Ezekiel describes the enemy, using the King of Tyre as a *type* (or foreshadowing) of Satan: "You were blameless in your ways from the day *you were created,* until unrighteousness was found in you" (Ezekiel 28:15).

Even though Satan and his demons are fallen angels, they don't have the same power or attributes as God. Dr. Wayne Grudem states, "The story of Job makes it clear that Satan could only do what God gave him permission to do and nothing more (Job 1:12; 2:6). Demons are kept in 'eternal chains' (Jude 6) and can be successfully resisted by Christians through the authority that Christ gives them (James 4:7). Moreover, the power of demons is limited. After rebelling against God, they do not have the power they had when they were angels, for sin is a weakening and destructive influence. The power of demons, though significant, is therefore probably less than the power of angels. In the area of knowledge, we should not think that demons can know the future or that they can read our minds or know our thoughts."[13]

We don't need to fear our enemy because God is vastly superior and more powerful than anything we can imagine. Indeed, His eternal kingdom will stand forever. By keeping our eyes on the eternal treasure, we can experience victory over sin. In order to reinforce this point, let's take a look now at *our* army.

It's important to remember that *God is the ultimate power of the universe.* The Old Testament contains wonderful examples of both kings and ordinary people believing in the power of God. When Sennacherib, pagan king of Assyria, boasted that he would conquer the land of Judah,

King Hezekiah responded by praising God for His greatness: "And Hezekiah prayed before the LORD and said, 'O LORD, the God of Israel, who art enthroned above the cherubim, Thou art the God, Thou alone, of all the kingdoms of the earth. Thou hast made heaven and earth'" (2 Kings 19:15).

After dedicating her first-born son Samuel to the Lord, Hannah prayed this beautiful prayer: "The LORD kills and makes alive; He brings down to Sheol and raises up. The LORD makes poor and rich; He brings low, He also exalts. He raises the poor from the dust, He lifts the needy from the ash heap to make them sit with nobles, and inherit a seat of honor; for the pillars of the earth are the LORD'S, and He set the world on them" (1 Samuel 2:6-8).

When the Moabites were coming to invade Judah, King Jehoshaphat stood in the courtyard and exclaimed, "O LORD, the God of our fathers, art Thou not God in the heavens? And art Thou not ruler over all the kingdoms of the nations? Power and might are in Thy hand so that no one can stand against Thee" (2 Chronicles 20:5, 6).

The Bible makes it clear that no one is equal to God. The leader of our army is the ruler of the entire universe. Under the control of God is a highly organized group of angels created by Him, in part, to minister to His saints. Dr. Grudem states, "Scripture clearly tells us that God sends angels for our protection…Angels also patrol the earth as God's representatives (Zechariah 1:10, 11) and carry out war against demonic forces."[14] The Word of God also helps explain the work of angels in our lives: "For He will give His angels charge concerning you, to guard you in all your ways" (Psalm 91:11). Our army consists of a universal ruler and angels who stand ready to guard and protect us as His saints.

There are also other tools at our disposal. Fellow Christians stand ready to help us. These people are a gold mine, but sometimes, we're too proud to use this resource. We're also afraid to expose ourselves to one another because our independent-minded culture makes it difficult for us to be vulnerable among members of the body of Christ. To avoid being judged, we put on our Sunday smile, shake a few hands, and go back to living our private hell.

Yet, you shouldn't let fear keep you from receiving the prayers, encouragement, and counsel from other Christians. There are many non-judgmental and loving brothers and sisters in the church whom the Lord longs for you to invite into your life. It would be wise for you to use this available resource. No one at Tim's church guessed that he was addicted to Internet pornography. Tim thought that if he let anyone know, he would be judged and condemned. He had assumed the worst by thinking that every man in the church would refuse to help him. He didn't give God a chance to work through his Christian brothers. If you want accountability in your life, begin to pray that God will provide loving Christians to walk with you.

This isn't to say that the Church should condone sin in its midst by looking the other way. This happens far too often in our churches as well. Church discipline was devised by God to restore wayward members back to an intimate relationship with God and to the body of Christ. Godly confrontation of sin includes love, with restoration as the goal. If no love is displayed, the troubled believer can be forced deeper into spiritual darkness because he now sees his Christian brothers and sisters as judges, not friends. He decides that the church is not on his side, so he moves out from under the umbrella that is meant to protect him. Instead of engaging in loving restoration, the church has judged this individual, which only drives him further away from Christ and into spiritual oblivion.

Living in a judgmental environment is no excuse for hiding your sin. You can reach out and ask for help, and then wait and watch. You'll find someone to help you. This takes courage, but remember, Christians are meant to minister to each other: "Iron sharpens iron, so one man sharpens another" (Proverbs 27:17). You'll be glad you took the risk.

The Holy Spirit is a resource that helps us gain victory over sin. In Galatians 5:16-25, Paul tells us that the power of the Holy Spirit is within all Christians. This passage helps us understand that we need to walk in the Spirit and not in the flesh.

The Bible (God's Word to us) is also a wonderful source of strength that helps us to overcome sin. Paul wrote these incredible words to Timothy: "All Scripture is inspired by God and profitable for teaching, for reproof, for correction, for training in righteousness; that the man of

God may be adequate, equipped for every good work" (2 Timothy 3:16, 17). We shouldn't underestimate the spiritual power that the Bible can exert upon our lives. God speaks directly to us through His Word. When we read Scripture in a systematic and meaningful way, the presence of the Holy Spirit will direct and guide us (Hebrews 4:12).

Prayer is another essential resource that God has given us so that we can "trade up." Communion with God should be the foundation of our effort to overcome sin. Promises regarding prayer (Matthew 7:7-11; Luke 18:1-8; John 5:14, 15; etc.) are found many places within the Bible. Also, Paul includes prayer as a necessary part of preparing for spiritual battle (Ephesians 6:18). Even though prayer is an essential key to experiencing victory over sin, many Christians see prayer as a duty rather than a privilege.

Wendi and I have been married for three years. In order to have an intimate relationship with her, I need to talk to her. Not only do I need to talk *at* her, but I also need to listen *to* her. Prayer can consist of a time of sharing our needs with God, but we should also include quiet meditation that allows us to hear His voice. When we are intimate with God, our lives are forever transformed.

When our lives change, we can *acknowledge eternity*. To overcome sin, we must live and breathe an eternal perspective. When we forget about the *bema*, the seductive invitations of the world overwhelm us.

On a recent trip to Las Vegas, I was saddened by what I observed. There were literally hundreds of strip clubs, exotic shows, bars, and gambling casinos. It's obvious that temporal pleasure is being purchased there in large quantities. Joy, however, is hard to find in Vegas. The city traps those who venture too close and offers nothing in return but broken cisterns. For the Christian, the site of a broken cistern should drive us back to the living water that Jesus offers.

Someday, we'll each stand before Christ. While we're saddened by Tim's computer addiction, we must understand that he will answer for every website that he's visited. The Lord is watching him today, and he must give an account later at the *bema*.

Having victory over sin requires an eternal mindset. Arlen L. Chitwood, a leading expert on the *bema*, writes, "Decisions and determinations emanating from the findings at the judgment seat will fall into two major categories—"Well done, thou good and faithful servant..." and "Thou wicked and slothful servant..." (cf. Matthew 25:19-30; Luke 19:15-26). The fact that "a just recompense"—exact payment for services rendered—will be meted out to every individual is set forth in Scripture in a number of different places through a number of different means (types, parables, direct statements), beginning with the writings of Moses in the Book of Genesis and terminating with the writings of John in the Book of Revelation. The Scriptures are replete with information concerning exactly what the future holds for all Christians, and there is no excuse for any Christian with an open Bible set before him to be other than knowledgeable concerning these things.

Each Christian will individually appear before the judgment seat of Christ to 'receive the things done in his body, according to that he hath done, whether it be good or bad.' The specific statement is made that Christians will be judged solely on the basis of that which they themselves have done, which will be judgment solely on the basis of works."[15]

Chitwood correctly reminds us that *there will be no excuse* at the Judgment Seat of Christ. This is not works-based righteousness because salvation has already been accomplished through Jesus' death on the cross. The *bema* involves what happens after salvation. This knowledge should be a deterrent to every believer who sees his sin as trivial. The eternal reality of the *bema* should sound an alarm inside of us each time we're tempted to rebel against Christ. There are no trivial or lesser sins; each one of our transgressions, though covered by the blood of Jesus and eternally dealt with regarding salvation, will be accounted for and will result in the loss of eternal rewards for faithful service on that great day of the believers' judgment.

⸻

This is the final and most important thing to remember: to have victory over sin, we must keep an eternal perspective. Joseph Dillow writes, "This, however, does not mean that we obey God only because it's our duty. That is the atheistic ethic, not the Christian one. The atheist maintains that good should be done only for the sake of good and with no reward for doing it. This is supposedly 'higher' than a Christian view. Yet the Scriptures repeatedly hold out eternal rewards as a central motivation for Christian living. When they are set in the context of gratitude for forgiveness of sins and the desire to say 'Thank you, Lord, for dying for me,' it is hard to see how this is selfish."[16] Dillow is absolutely correct.

In my car's rearview mirror, the outside temperature appears in a small box. I cannot look at my mirror without being reminded that it's hot outside. In the same way, eternity stares at us directly in the face. We can develop a thought process that allows eternity to be an ever-present *box* in the mirror of our thought life. It's then that we have a wonderful opportunity to overcome sin and truly "trade up."

—

Linda had missed her quiet time again this morning. *It's all right,* she thought, *God isn't legalistic.* She pulled into her parking space at work. If Linda knew what was about to happen, her attitude about spending time with Christ would be a little less nonchalant.

The young woman gave a cursory glance at the security guard. Linda turned right past the information desk and approached large glass doors emblazoned with the "Triad Corporation" logo. "Triad," she mumbled. "Just another financial firm in a world full of financial firms, each trying to outguess each other to make a few extra bucks. Maybe, someday I'll even meet a client."

The office came to life as Linda walked through a row of cubicles. As always, she turned her computer on and headed for the coffee machine. The coffee was bad, but at least it contained caffeine.

She guided herself quickly past her co-workers, trying to avoid eye contact. Linda wasn't a morning person. The last thing she wanted right now was some trivial conversation about her plans for the weekend. She had work to do and wanted to finish on time.

Linda grabbed a foam cup and poured it full of very black coffee. No cream and sugar today: she wanted to get started. Today would be a normal Friday. Weekends meant a lot to her. She would work through lunch if she had to, since every minute was precious.

A hand grabbed her elbow as she returned to her desk. Her heart sank as she turned around to see Phil Blankston, the Senior Vice-President for Marketing. She and Phil had what could be called a "rocky" relationship, and this was no way to start the morning.

"Oh, Phil, how are you?" she asked, trying to sound sincere.

"Not good. I need to see you in my office right now," Phil blurted out as he started toward his corner office near the restrooms. Linda knew that this was not a request, but an order. Mumbling profanity under her breath, Linda followed Phil into his office. She sat down and he closed the door.

Phil began, "Linda, I'm in big trouble."

"What's wrong?"

The senior VP paced by the corner window that provided a breath-taking view of the Pittsburgh skyline. "I've really screwed up, and I need your help."

Linda felt a queasy feeling come over her. "Okay, tell me about it," she replied.

"I have a client…his name is Martin…runs a dry-cleaning business downtown." Phil sat down in his chair but didn't face Linda. "He came to see me last Friday. He said that he wanted to invest fifty-thousand in a high-yield fund. I told him that I wouldn't be able to get the money in until the following Monday morning, so I held it for him."

"That's no big deal. I've done that before," Linda said.

"No…it's a big deal. You see, well, Linda, can I trust you with this?"

Now, she really didn't feel well but managed to squeeze out a yes. "What's the problem, Phil?"

"I used a…well…let's just say…a portion of the money over last weekend."

"What? How….why?"

"He gave me forty-five grand in a cashier's check and another five thousand in cash from the week's receipts. Linda, I used the five thousand. I've been hoping to see a stock rise on the Dow in order to pay him back, but it hasn't happened. He thinks I already invested that money. I don't have $5,000."

"Where did it all go?" Linda demanded as she approached the desk and turned his chair toward her.

"Debt."

"What kind of debt?"

"A gambling debt."

"What!" Linda was incredulous.

"I play some sports bets…no big deal, but I owed somebody and…"

"And now you want me to give you the money and pretend none of this ever happened. How close am I, Phil?"

There was an awkward moment of silence as Linda waited for Phil to respond. "Could you? I'm good for it. You know I'll give it back to you in a couple of weeks. If you could just float me the money, Martin will never know what happened."

Linda paced the room. She stopped and looked directly at him. "You're asking me to violate every ethical standard that I have, not to mention the fact that I should report you to the proper officials. I won't do it."

For the first time, Phil became angry. He startled Linda as he jumped from his chair and pointed his finger in her face. "Linda, I don't want to remind you that I really don't have to ask you. You do this for me now, or you will be gone in a day. How dare you say no to me! You'll either help me or you're gone. Do you understand?"

Linda slumped into a chair and thought about her predicament. He was right; he could fire her on the spot. She desperately tried to remember Bible verses that could help her now, but she was completely alone. It was just her and the VP. She couldn't afford to lose this job because of her family responsibilities. She didn't feel good about any of this. She'd always been a Christian and had always tried to follow ethical standards. She'd made her share of mistakes, so how could she hold Phil to a higher standard than the one she held for herself? Even though she was feeling sick all over, she knew that her career was at stake. "Okay," she said. "What do you want me to do?"

Linda's quest for temporal satisfaction took on these forms:

- Her desire to keep her job above all else
- Her failure to think through the consequences of what she was about to do

- Her failure to trust God to take care of her if she did get fired
- Her failure to be armed for battle: she'd neglected her time with Christ
- Her failure to memorize Bible verses that would help her when temptation came.

A temptation came to her with no warning and from an unexpected place. The obvious sin is Linda's willingness to violate her ethical standards in order to keep her job. Under the surface, there is also a fear of the unknown, a lack of trust in God, and a lack of intimacy with Christ. Courage that comes from knowing God would've helped her navigate this sticky situation.

Earlier in this chapter, we met Tim, who was stationed at his computer. For him, this was the worst night of all. While his family slept, he had looked at some of the most vile images he'd ever seen. He turned off his computer and walked outside. The things he'd just witnessed cascaded through his mind. He literally shook his head and wondered if he could ever be clean and pure again. He wondered if he could ever look at his wife in the same way again.

His pace quickened as he became angry at himself and God. In the darkness he screamed, "Lord, why won't you help me?" He had hit bottom. Sitting down on the curb he sobbed for what seemed like hours. He was alone, and it seemed that all hope was gone.

Tim's quest for temporal satisfaction took on these forms:

- His pain that he dealt with through Internet pornography rather than through the Lord Jesus Christ
- His unwillingness to find the holes that pornography was temporarily filling in his life
- His unwillingness to see the temporal and eternal consequences of his sin
- His selfish desire to do what pleased him, no matter how much it hurt the people around him.

What about you? You can begin to have victory over sin by answering the following questions:

1. What are the broken cisterns in my life?
2. Where am I the most vulnerable to satanic attack?
3. Is my relationship with God such that I understand the army that stands with me?
4. Have I really understood the eternal and temporal consequences of my sin?
5. Is there one sin in my life that is becoming a *besetting* or a *habitual* sin? If so, am I going to do something about it?
6. Do I trust God enough to confront my sin?

Notes:

_____

_____

_____

_____

_____

_____

_____

_____

_____

_____

_____

_____

_____

_____

A Prayer to Have Victory Over Sin:

Lord, help me to be disgusted with sin. Show me the vile, selfish, and ugly nature of my sin and the temporal and eternal damage that is caused by it. Teach me to hate sin and see sin the way you see it. Remind me of the army that stands ready to assist me in battle. Please help me to learn how to access the power of the Holy Spirit. Teach me to identify the lies of the enemy. Free me from bondage and help me learn to trust You more. It's in You that I trust. Amen.

*"Not everyone who says to Me on that day, 'Lord, Lord,' will
enter the kingdom of heaven; but he who does the will of
My Father who is in heaven. Many will say to Me on that day,
'Lord, Lord, did we not prophesy in Your name, and in
Your name cast out demons, and in Your name perform
many miracles?' And then I will declare to them,
'I never knew you; depart from Me, you who practice lawlessness.'*

Matthew 7:21-23

10. Janet Chismar, ed. "Combating Internet Pornography - Part 2", *News & Culture*, 2006, www.crosswalk.com.

11. Morton C. Orman, M.D. *A Special Report by Morton C. Orman, M.D.,* 1996, www.stresscure.com.

12. Anthony A. Hoekema.. *Created in God's Image.* (Carlisle, UK: the Paternoster Press-Eerdmans, 1986), 141.

13. Wayne Grudem, *Systematic Theology.* (Grand Rapids: Zondervan. 1994), 415.

14. *Grudem, Systematic Theology,* 399; 404.

15. Arlen L. Chitwood, *The Judgment Seat of Christ* (Norman: The Lamp Broadcast, Inc.,1986), 35-36.

16. Joseph C. Dillow, *The Reign of the Servant Kings: A Study of Eternal Security and the Final Significance of Man.* (Hayesville: Schoettle, 1992), 529.

5 When I *Trade Up* I Can Experience a New and Vital Christian Life!

The hospital room was bleak and cold. Jodee sat on top of one bed; the other sat empty, near the window. I looked around and noticed the light-blue bedding and white walls. Two small television sets jutted out toward each bed. The blinds on the window were closed, and the bright fluorescent lights added a harsh reality to the unwelcoming surroundings.

This is a strange place to do the test, I thought to myself as we waited for the doctor to see us. *You'd think there'd be someone waiting for us. At least someone should be here to ask Jodee how she's feeling.* But we were alone, and my heart was in turmoil. My wife probably had cancer; we were about to find out one way or the other.

After what seemed like years, a doctor in her mid-thirties scurried into the room. She seemed kind, and her warm smile helped ease the loneliness for a short while. But the feeling of warmth didn't last.

She began by asking my wife the usual questions. A mammogram had detected a lump in her breast earlier in the week. Jodee seemed to be doing well, so she had calmly gone about her business. It's almost if she knew that the worst was about to come, but she was somehow able to keep her emotions in check.

As a nurse, Jodee knew how to read body language. After her mammogram was read, she noticed tension in their faces. She was immediately scheduled to have a biopsy performed. My wife sensed that things were not good, and she was right.

The young doctor quickly went to work. She pulled out the largest needle that I'd ever seen, and it made my stomach queasy just to look at it. She walked over to Jodee and plunged it into her left breast. I held Jodee's hand as she winced and smiled. *That's courage,* I thought to myself as the needle was withdrawn.

I expected the doctor to leave the room and re-enter with heart-stopping news, but things were hardly that dramatic. She simply walked over to the counter and emptied the syringe into a Petri dish. She carefully peered at the material through a microscope. We anxiously awaited her diagnosis.

We were at the mercy of a doctor we'd never met, while wondering if our lives were going to change forever. I remember thinking that this was all some kind of unreal nightmare because Jodee was not the sickly kind. She was a strong woman who worked hard. In fact, I'd never doubted that she would outlive me, but that presupposition was about to change.

Finally, the doctor pulled away from the microscope and made her way to the bed with the news. I wasn't shocked by what I heard. "I am sorry, you do have cancer," the doctor said while I held Jodee's hand. "I will give the results to your doctor, and he will be in touch shortly."

Just like that, a few short words changed our lives, forever affecting my children, family, and friends. Jodee Jean Johnson had breast cancer: the truth was beginning to sink in.

Our first priority was to tell the children. We had already decided that it would be best to be upfront with them. After telling them the truth with gentleness, God would do the rest. With heavy hearts, we headed for home. My parents were visiting, so they would be there too. I didn't feel well because it was my responsibility to tell three children that their mother had cancer. Adina was only fifteen, Jeremy thirteen, and Taylor was ten. This wasn't going to be easy.

I asked Jodee how she was doing as I parked the car in the driveway, and she said she was okay. We agreed that we were going to tell everyone the truth—no more and no less. We would tell them that there was hope for a complete recovery, but I wouldn't conceal the fact that Jodee's life was threatened.

After calling the family together, we all met in our family room. I remember standing against the counter with Jodee. The other five family members were standing in a semi-circle, staring directly at me. I said a quick prayer and then blurted out the news: "Guys, we just found out that your mom has breast cancer." I waited for any tears or screams, but there were none. I continued, "We just learned that she has a lump that is cancerous, so we're going to see a doctor right away. If we caught it early, there's a good chance that she'll be all right. I just wanted to tell you now so you know what's going on. I want you to know that during this entire process we'll be totally honest with you. There'll be no secrets, so you can ask us any questions at any time."

I stopped and looked around. There was deep concern, but no panic. The boys were silent, but Adina started to cry. My mom and dad went over to comfort her. I felt empty inside. Afraid to lose Jodee, I wondered if my faith could handle this. After breaking the sad news, walking out of the room was all I was capable of doing. The truth was out, and a difficult process had begun.

A few days later, we met with our oncologist for the first time; he would tell us how bad it was. At this point, I was still confident that everything would be all right. Most women win the battle against breast cancer. At thirty-eight, Jodee was relatively young and strong, so she could certainly beat this. There was no way Jodee was going to die; it just didn't make any sense.

We waited in a room filled with cancer patients, and more of the reality set in. Most of them had no hair, while others had yellow skin as the result of severe liver cancer. Some were young and some were old, but they all had one thing in common: cancer.

We sat down and talked with the doctor, whom I liked immediately. Dr. Schwartz was a no-nonsense straight-shooter, but he still cared about his patients. Unfortunately, he was also the bearer of bad news: the cancer was aggressive. We all agreed to treat it as such, since there was no reason to fool around. We were going to win, so we wanted to get started immediately.

Jodee's care team set up a plan. The first step would involve two weeks of chemotherapy to try shrinking the tumor, after which surgery would be performed. They would try to avoid a total mastectomy. There was no turning back now.

During this time, I began to lose my spiritual footing. My world began to spin out of control. I was feeling tired, angry, and helpless all at the same time. Often, I went nose to nose with God, screaming, "Why Jodee?" He could handle my pain as I desperately reached out to Him. I felt lost and bewildered, because cancer was not part of my life plan.

Meanwhile, Jodee's treatment continued for the next couple of weeks. The tumor had been reduced by the chemo, and the follow-up surgery was also successful. They were able to save most of her breast. There would be another round of chemo, along with a two-week period of radiation treatment, after which we would get back to life as we knew it. Hope once again returned to the Johnson household: Jodee wasn't going to die. She would survive, as most women did.

My newfound hope was short-lived, however, because the lymph nodes were involved. While this wasn't a good sign, because it's the lymph nodes that usually send the cancer to various parts of the body, an MRI showed no movement of the cancer. Fortunately, it hadn't latched onto the lungs or liver. The aggressive treatment would continue, and then it would be over.

Jodee's illness was the talk of the church. She gave a beautiful testimony of her faith in Christ, but her battle soon became a public spectacle. When I walked on the church campus, I heard many kind words that echoed through my head, along with questions about Jodee's health. Although I appreciated their concern, I was still hurting. Talking about it just made it worse, so I wanted to hide. In my mind, the well-wishers had gone too far, and I felt like my privacy had been invaded. At one point, I remember even feeling a literal physical pain in my chest

I thought I had to keep my best face on, as an example for all to see. At the same time, I was receiving terrible pressure from my senior pastor. One day, he called me into his office and said, "Paul, we're counting on you to show us how to love a woman." I was stunned. How dare he! He had no idea about what I was going through. It was not up to me to show anyone anything. I was responsible for loving my wife and my family, and God would show me how.

During this period of time, I began to crawl deep into myself by avoiding contact with friends and members of my church. My pain was so great that words were no longer sufficient. In order to survive, I became superficial, giving pat answers to difficult questions. I was dying inside, but no one knew it.

Jodee finally completed her full regimen of chemo and radiation and received a graduation certificate from her doctor's office. It was finally over; Jodee had beaten cancer. The doctor said that we should treat the cancer as a chronic disease that could reappear at some point, but we didn't care. Five years seemed like an eternity after what we'd been through.

Our lives returned to normal for a few weeks until Jodee started feeling pain in her lower back. We immediately went back to the doctor, who guessed that Jodee had slipped a disc. To make sure, a routine MRI was scheduled.

I was having lunch with my friend Gary when my cell phone rang. It was Dr. Schwartz. He said, "Paul, I wanted to call you first. Jodee's cancer has spread throughout her body. It's in her spine and her brain. You need to see your radiologist right away." I was so glad I was with Gary at the time, because we had shared so many things. It was no coincidence that this call came during one of our lunches. I said, "Gary, the doctor said that Jodee's cancer has metastasized all over her body. Now, I have to go home and tell Jodee and the kids." Gary prayed for me, and I headed home.

I called the family together, and they immediately knew something was wrong because I didn't do a very good job of hiding my emotions. First, I took Jodee into the bedroom to tell her the bad news. I wasn't very good at doing this kind of thing. How many times does a husband tell her wife that her body is filled with cancer? I said, "Jodee, I'm so sorry. Dr. Schwartz called and said that the pain in your back was not a slipped disc. It's cancer. There's cancer in your bones, in your kidney, and in your brain. I'm sorry. I wish there was a better way to say it. We need to see your radiologist tomorrow." I held her, but she didn't cry. We walked out to tell the kids, and they cried.

The next day, we sat in front of the radiologist. I will never forget what he said because it was so honest. He remarked, "It would be an understatement to say that this is shitty." We smiled. "Your cancer is terminal," he told Jodee. "All we can do now is try to make you comfortable. I can do radiation or Dr. Schwartz can do chemotherapy. You have to decide." I asked him how long Jodee had to live, and he replied that it would be two years, tops. The roof caved in, and my life was a thick, confusing fog. Jodee was going to die. We went home to tell the children, and they cried again.

The emotional pain I experienced over the next few months was almost unbearable. I couldn't sleep because I was constantly taking care of Jodee. I often stayed up late at night to make sure that she took the proper medicine. She was taking chemo treatments for a while to give her some comfort, but when Dr. Schwartz noticed her shivering in his office, he told her to stop. He kindly told her that he had done everything he could do. He's a good man who cares about his patients. Some time after she had passed away, he sent me a note of sympathy.

I was a mess, filled with the pain of losing my wife of 20+ years. My mind ran wild with thoughts like, *maybe God is getting me out of a hard marriage.* I felt relief, and then the guilt quickly set in. *How can you think of such a thing? You're a pig!* I told myself. I often thought, *are there any other women out there?* The guilt and shame of thinking such a thought came crashing over me like thunder. My thought life was out of control.

At the same time, I was angry with God. No, those words are too kind: I hated God because He was taking the mother of my children away from them. I might be able to get remarried and move on with my life, but my children only had one mother. *How could you do that, God?* my thoughts screamed out. *Where is Your love and mercy?*

Now, as I look back, I realize that He was there nearby—comforting, steering, providing, and protecting me. In fact, a good friend of mine said she saw an angel in our home, and I believe her. I know now that God never left us.

As Jodee's condition worsened, I began to get my spiritual feet back under me. I started to read a book to her about heaven, realizing that soon Jodee would be there. I wanted to take care of her, but soon I wouldn't be able to anymore.

Because Jodee's brain tumor was starting to affect her, strange things began to happen to her. She fell out of bed on a regular basis. Sometimes, she stared at me blankly. Other times she would angrily tell me that I was no good to her and accuse me of having affairs with other women. I struggled to tell myself that these were just the effects of the cancer. It wasn't Jodee that was talking, but it still hurt. I knew the time was coming when I would have to bring her into hospice care because I couldn't protect her anymore.

Meanwhile, I withdrew deeper and deeper into myself. The church had given me a leave of absence. Many well-meaning Christians suggested Internet sites with new-found cures. *Do you think I'm stupid? Do you not think I've researched every possible option and found the best doctors available? Leave me alone,* I shouted from inside my head.

Jodee was dying, and her time was getting close. My raw faith was on God's refining table. My relationship with Christ was no longer filled with trivial Christian solutions: I was on the firing line. Either God was or wasn't who He claimed to be. I trusted that He was and clung to Him for dear life, believing that God was in control. I knew Jodee would be healed in Heaven. The more I focused on eternity, which was what really mattered, the more I found joy, even in the darkest hours of my life. I discovered that amid this turmoil and pain, I could experience a victorious Christian life.

The day finally came when I made the hardest decision of my life. Jodee would need full-time hospice care. My hands shook as I managed to pick up the phone. The person at the other end of the line listened and sent an ambulance to my house. Our friend Nancy was there. My kids were in the front yard, crying. I pretended to be in control, but I was really dying on the inside. *Jodee will never come back,* I thought. *She'll never see her home again. This is good-bye.* After the ambulance left, I told the kids to get their shoes on. Then, I went inside the house and cried.

Her stay in hospice was less than a week. I would arrive each morning and spend the day at her bedside. We talked when she was lucid, but she slept most of the time. I still remember watching my wife of twenty years for hours. I was helpless to do anything, so I felt worthless.

There were some good times in hospice, however. When Jodee

couldn't speak, she would lift her right arm and move her fingers. That's how she said "hi." I waved back, and we both smiled.

On one particular morning, I arrived at 9. Jodee was sitting on top of the bed and looked great. I asked her how she was feeling, and she replied that she was doing better. Then, she laid down on her right side. I knelt at the side of the bed and told her that I loved her. She said she loved me too. I thanked her for putting up with me for twenty years. She smiled and said, "You too." Then, she fell asleep and didn't wake up again.

I'm thankful for that last moment together because it gave us emotional closure. God blessed us with it out of His compassionate grace. It was good to say and hear those words. Jodee was going to die, but at least I said *I love you* one last time.

As the week of her death progressed, our friends and family visited often until I finally sent everyone home. (The nurse told me that the distractions made it hard for Jodee to die.) Only Jodee's family and close friends remained. My children sang one of the most beautiful things I've ever heard in a circle around Jodee's bed. Songs of praise to God echoed through the hallways of the hospice. They were only teenagers, but they stared Satan right in the face, saying in effect, *death doesn't defeat us.* Their courageous singing during this difficult time is an inspiring memory that will always stay with me. The nurses couldn't have missed the powerful message that my children delivered by praising God, either. They had to know that these people loved Jesus. Finally, I sent my children home because I didn't want them to watch their mother die.

The nurse said Jodee was a fighter who didn't want to let go. Most young mothers want to live in order to stay and protect their children. Jodee hung on until early afternoon. Eight of us waited by her bedside. Her mother held her hand. I didn't need to, because it was more important for her to do it at that special time. They loved each other very much. I just stood on the side of the room, making sure everyone was holding up all right. The morning dragged on.

Jodee's breathing became more shallow over time. Watching someone die is not pretty. She was struggling, so I prayed that God would ease her pain. Now was the time for her to go and be with Jesus. Finally, she took her last breath, and I screamed in a loud voice, "Jodee is with Jesus!" I felt joy when I thought of the Lord's arms wrapping around her. Even though I couldn't take care of her anymore, Jesus could. I felt a strong sense of relief because Jodee had gone home to be with the Lord, where she belonged.

An hour later, I went into her room. Nancy was gently removing her earrings. The body was there, but Jodee wasn't. I left before they came to get her. I hadn't slept in four days, but sleep just wouldn't come. I had never felt so empty in all my life. My heart literally hurt as I felt our marriage *oneness* being torn apart. The pain went all the way down to the marrow of my bones. I lay in bed and thought about the future.

So many challenges were ahead. *How am I going to get my kids through this? How can I live with this pain? Where is God?* There were many questions but little sleep. It wasn't for another year that I could sleep without background television noise because of my ongoing heartache and pain.

It'd be difficult for me to live a victorious Christian life because I was so emotionally and spiritually vulnerable. The world's medications offered many ways to ease the pain, and over time, they became more enticing. I wanted to be through with the pain, so I considered sex, drinking, and suicide. Realizing that no easy formula would erase the pain, I turned to God, who is good all the time. The Holy Spirit gave me discernment to avoid Satan's minefields.

God was showing me how to have victory in my Christian life by using the scars of Jodee's death. I've discovered that He often uses pain to produce growth in the life of a believer. Pain is God's road to glory.

Many biblical heroes suffered in extreme ways. Job suffered. Jacob limped. Joseph was abandoned. Paul was tested. The apostles were beaten. Many times, this has been the Lord's plan for His people.

When we're in pain, we have two choices: to run or be still. If we run, we'll miss God. Escaping from pain just can't happen, and we won't be able to learn the life lessons that will bring us eternal rewards. When we sit still, on the other hand, we'll experience God in a new way by learning how to trust Him and then doing those things that will offer eternal treasure. In short, He becomes our closest friend.

Few Christians are still when they experience hardship; in fact, most of them will run away. New homes, higher salaries, more children, pornography, and emotional affairs are just some of the ways that are commonly used to flee. We think that we can escape from the pain, but that's a demonic lie. If we try to run away, the pain will track us down sooner or later, eventually destroying our spirituality and cutting off our opportunity to be victorious in the Christian life. But, we can learn to see pain and suffering differently—as a friend, not an enemy. We have to choose. Are we going to allow pain to transform us or are we going to run away and stay the way we are?

When we keep our eyes on eternity, pain becomes an asset. Jesus taught His disciples that eternal treasure and suffering go together: "If anyone wishes to come after me, let him deny himself, and take up his cross and follow Me. For whoever wishes to save his life will lose it; but whoever loses his life for My sake and the gospel's shall save it" (Mark 8:34, 35).

The point that Jesus made is clear. Experiencing victory in the Christian life requires us to follow Him at all costs. This will likely mean that we'll be uncomfortable at times. Oswald Chambers noted, "We all know people who have been made much meaner and more irritable and more intolerable to live with by suffering: it's not right to say that all suffering perfects. It only perfects one type of person…the one who accepts the call of God in Christ Jesus."[17] Which type of person are you?

Today's Christians like to be comfortable. Fewer and fewer pastors are teaching that sacrifice is an essential part of the Christian life. Soft teaching about the love of Christ without any regard for foundational theology is the norm. Pastors grow mega-churches by sharing only half of the gospel message. They "dumb down" sermons for their listeners by only talking about the comfortable side of the Christian life. They assure their members that God doesn't want them to suffer. They buy into this kind of teaching and churches grow. Everyone smiles, and all seems well. This just amounts to what I call "Christian Cruise Control." Only *this* life is in view; eternity has been forgotten.

There is another part of the gospel message that's increasingly hard to find in our modern churches: self-denial. Ironically, this neglected portion of the Lord's teaching can lead to a new and vital life, along with eternal rewards. Selflessness will be greatly honored at the *bema*. Who in their right mind would trade a little bit of earthly comfort for treasure in eternity? But we all do it. When we make selfish decisions, we fail to "trade up."

Sometimes, others show us what it means to think about something bigger than ourselves. Charlie Weis, the head football coach at the University of Notre Dame, used to be the offensive coordinator for the New England Patriots. Considered by many to be a genius, he called all of the plays—that is, until he met little Montana Mazurkiewicz. Montana, named after famed Notre Dame quarterback Joe Montana, was ten years old and dying because of a brain tumor.

One day, Montana asked if one of the Notre Dame football players would come and visit him, since he lived just a few miles from the stadium. Instead of sending a player, Coach Weis himself came to his door. The burly coach and the tiny boy spent time together that day. When Weis was ready to leave, he asked Montana, "Is there anything else I can do?" Montana quickly responded, "I would like to call a play. Not just any play, but a pass to the right on the first play of the game." Weis agreed.

Montana died a day and a half later. The following Saturday, the Fighting Irish played a difficult game against Michigan. After a miscue on the opening kick-off, Weis' team was on its own one-yard line. Even though nobody passes on the one-yard line, Weis said later that he told his assistants he had no choice but to honor Montana's request. The quarterback threw a short pass to the right for a first down. Charlie Weis realized then that there were more important things besides football. He honored a sick boy and his family by keeping his word. Even though the coach didn't want the story to come out, ESPN aired it, inspiring thousands of people.

What Charlie Weis did that day in Ann Arbor, Michigan, was not comfortable for him. He risked an interception or a fumble near his own goal line in order to do the right thing. A "cruise control Christian," however, will always strive to be comfortable. This person will most likely never experience any depth in his relationship with Christ. He will be like a child who is content to play in the sand with no thought for the future. Adult maturity is never reached because, for the child, the sand-box becomes eternity.

The Christian child who is willing to step out of life's sandbox will experience a new level of existence. He may get dirty. There may be holes in the ground that will twist his ankles. But life in its truest form, with all of its best and worst, will be experienced. Enduring life's pitfalls is the best way to grow. This child matures and discovers a better life, with adulthood as the reward.

A new and vital Christian life can only be found inside the bounds of an intimate relationship with Jesus. The formula is simple: all of us experience pain, but self-denial comes when we stay still. By doing this, we learn more about Christ and develop a more intimate relationship with Him in which we discover a new and vital Christian life.

Comfort and self-satisfaction don't lead to a vital relationship with Jesus. God has not promised smooth sailing for His children. The soft-selling pulpiteers of our day are lying; embracing suffering is the only way to find new life. There is no escape from pain, only the *illusion* of escape. Our selfish desires must be destroyed in order to pave the way for a deeper relationship with Jesus. When self is denied and a closer fellow-ship with Christ is gained in the process, we have "traded up."

—

Gwen didn't like the emptiness she felt in her belly, even though her life at first glance seemed full. She was on her way to church with her hus-band at the wheel of the family mini-van. Her three beautiful children filled the second and third rows of seats. She considered herself fortunate. Her husband was a good guy. He was handsome, and the gray hair around his temples added a new hint of respectability.

Gwen considered herself to be a pretty woman. The ladies at church fawned over her and often paid her compliments on her clothing and hairstyle. She smiled each time. A glance in the van's sunshade mirror confirmed what she already knew. Bright green eyes, highlighted by sandy-blond hair and soft skin, concealed her real age. She had it all.

What was this empty feeling inside of her, then? It felt as if something was missing. If Gwen wasn't a Christian, she would have understood, realizing that unbelievers had a hole in their heart which could only be filled with Christ. She was a Christian, so this hole wasn't supposed to be there. Yet, she couldn't quite put her finger on the problem.

The van pulled into the church parking lot. Smiling attendants pointed the family to an open spot not far from the education building. *This is a good place to park,* she thought. *God was watching out for them today.* It was just like the pastor had said last Sunday: "God prefers you because you are His sons and daughters. Just pray and He will give you what you ask for." *He had even mentioned parking spaces,* she remembered. The thought made her smile.

Gwen and her husband safely escorted their children to their Sunday school rooms. The couple stopped by the coffee bar and ordered lattes— hers with just a touch of vanilla. She liked it here.

The worship service was just starting. Gwen grabbed a bulletin from a smiling greeter. She scanned the worship center; the place was huge. She had heard about their numbers, something like twenty-thousand in attendance per Sunday. That seemed about right. The auditorium was full again today, but two chairs were open near the side aisle. *God prefers us,* she thought. The couple took their seats. For the moment, the emptiness had subsided.

The worship band began to play, and the congregation came to life. Two huge screens showed words and pictures. A roving camera revealed close-up shots of worshippers caught up in heavenly sounds. The young, talented musicians sang praise songs about love. Glad that Jesus loved her, Gwen began to sing.

The pastor was dressed in a tailored blue suit today. *He is a handsome man,* Gwen thought as she sat back to enjoy the sermon. The talented communicator knew how to keep the attention of his audience. He was a great storyteller who didn't need to hold his Bible. This morning's message was based on 1 John 3:11: "For this is the message which you have heard from the beginning, that we should love one another." Gwen laughed at the pastor's jokes and listened to his engaging tales. After hearing the sermon, she decided that she should try to be a kinder person.

Gwen reflected on the service as the van pulled away from the church. While the family was heading to a fast-food place for lunch, the

emptiness in her soul returned. As she fumbled through her purse for lip-
stick, an object fell on the floor mat. She recognized the booklet as a gift
from a close friend. Its title read *Meditations for a Deeper Walk*. Her friend
had written a note on the inside of the cover. It read, "Gwen, I'm praying for you. Don't be afraid to let God take you deeper. I hope this book
helps you find your joy. Love, Suzie."

Gwen flipped through the small book. Each page contained a
thought and a Bible verse. *When was the last time I read the Bible? Does
my emptiness come from a lack of joy?* Gwen was quiet during the ride
home because she had plenty to think about.

Gwen's quest for temporal satisfaction took on these forms:

- Her unwillingness to deal with an increasing emptiness
- Her willingness to settle for soft teaching
- Her refusal to seek more depth in her relationship with Christ
- Her willingness to rely on her beauty and her family's success to
  find joy.

Gwen is like millions of us Christians who seek the most appealing
things in life, but they are not always the best things. Satan's trap for us
has been set. We can seek a vital and victorious life on the most appealing road, but this route only leads into an empty desert wilderness. We
need to "trade up" by immersing ourselves in the way of Christ. Even
though His way will most likely not be easy, it is the one that leads to ful-
fillment and glory.

What about you? You can begin to live a vital and victorious
Christian life when you ask yourself the following questions:

1. Do I receive solid Bible teaching each week? Does my pastor usually
   do topical messages, or does he preach through the books of the
   Bible? How often do I open my Bible in church?
2. Why do I attend my church?
3. What do I give back to my church?
4. What is the pain that is active in my life?
5. Have I embraced the pain, or do I run from it?

6. What methods do I use to medicate pain?
7. Is my relationship with Christ worth total sacrifice?
8. Am I with God for the long haul, or am I riding the fence?
9. Have I been honest with myself while answering these questions?

Notes:

_____

_____

_____

_____

_____

_____

_____

_____

A Prayer for a New and Vital Christian Life:

Lord, teach me to see pain as a friend. Show me how I can learn from pain. Bring suffering into my life if it will help me become more like You. I submit to You. I want to know more about You and learn to love You deeply. Take away the things that keep me from You and teach me to see the things that will help me grow. I love You. Amen.

"The thief comes only to steal and kill and destroy;
I came that they might have life, and might have it abundantly."

John 10:10

---

17. Oswald Chambers, *My Utmost for His Highest* (Uhrichsville, OH: Barbour Publishing, Inc., 1935-c1992), 193.

6 When I *Trade Up* I Can Be Free to Love Others and Myself!

The Gospel of Luke records one of the most stunning accounts in all of Scripture. Jesus told a story that was meant to touch all of us. In the well-known parable of the prodigal son, we receive insight into God's unconditional forgiveness. It's a glimpse of what's waiting for us when we repent, as well as a taste of eternal rewards.

This parable features a discontented young man whose family wealth didn't satisfy his heart. He was determined to find out what the world had to offer him instead; so he ran away from home. His father must have wondered if he would ever see him again. It must have been very difficult to watch his son walk away, yet he knew that the boy would find out what the real world was like and learn many lessons along the way.

His traveling money didn't last long because he chased after all of the pleasure that he could find. It didn't end well: he found himself in the sty, eating with pigs to survive. Even though the world's cisterns failed to satisfy his heart, the boy wondered if he could ever return to his old life. Would he be accepted back? He was prepared for the worst by being willing to become a paid servant in his father's household. Luke's account of Jesus' parable reads, "But when he came to his senses, he said, 'How many of my father's hired men have more than enough bread, but I am dying here with hunger! I will get up and go to my father, and will say to him, "Father, I have sinned against heaven, and in your sight; I am no longer worthy to be called your son; make me as one of your hired men'" (Luke 15:17-19).

Zane Hodges, the famous Bible scholar, gives us this insight: "This was a good decision. But it was flawed. His father was not interested in making the bargain his son was thinking about. His dad was prepared to receive him freely. His love for his prodigal boy was not conditioned on any kind of pledge to serve on the farm. Restoring harmony with his father was going to be ever so much easier than he had imagined. The story of the prodigal son therefore is not simply a story about salvation. It's a story about how a long-separated father and son were reunited. It's a story about a dad who did much more than take his boy back. In fact it's a story about how a father lavished his love on an erring son and sat down with him, in fellowship, at a splendid and joyous banquet. Unmistakably, the story of the prodigal son is the story of the sinner's restoration to fellowship with God our heavenly Father. But repentance is always about that, even when the repenting sinner is already a Christian!"[18]

Forgiveness was offered at no charge. This boy received unconditional love from his father, despite his sinful actions. In fact, the father gave his son a precious ring representing his inheritance and a held a large banquet in honor of his return. Jesus used this parable to illustrate His merciful love for us. He will forgive us for any crime; this is a poignant biblical truth. First John 1:9 reassures us that, "If we confess our sins, He is faithful and righteous to forgive us our sins and to cleanse us from all unrighteousness." Could John have meant *all* unrighteousness? Is John referring to *my* sinful behavior and horrible past? Yes. Christ offers complete forgiveness to His children. This is a difficult concept to understand and accept; however, if we can't receive God's unconditional love, we won't be free to love others, nor find the strength to love ourselves.

Tucson is full of spectacular canyons and mountain views. On the hillside of one such canyon is a pathway signifying the Stations of the Cross. This Roman Catholic ritual of contrition involves the reenactment of the traditional stages in Jesus' journey to his death. The Catholic Encyclopedia explains: "In conclusion it may be safely asserted that there is no devotion more richly endowed with *indulgences* (in the special sense

where it is used here, an indulgence is a remission of the temporal punishment due to *sin*, the guilt of which has been forgiven) than the
Stations of the Cross, and none which enables us more literally to obey
Christ's injunction to take up our cross and follow Him."[19] In other
words, taking part in this ritual is intended to solicit God's forgiveness of
sin.

While this can be an important devotional exercise for many pil-
grims, its hypothesis is incorrect. We can't earn forgiveness and love from
God because these are God's gifts to us. Paul made this point abundantly
clear in his letter to the Romans: "For the wages of sin is death, but the
free gift of God is eternal life in Christ Jesus our Lord" (Romans 6:23).
Forgiveness and love are free gifts from God. We can learn to pass these
gifts on to others, but something that isn't received can't be passed on.

Focusing our eyes on eternity can help us understand and receive
God's free gift. At the *bema*, we'll be accountable for our service to
Jesus—not our salvation. We can forgive ourselves by understanding the
unshakable certainty of salvation. When we forgive ourselves first, then
we can forgive others. In other words, when there's forgiveness, there also
can be love.

There is forgiveness because of what Jesus did for us on the cross. It's
important to remember that the *bema* won't decide our salvation. The
crucifixion and resurrection of Jesus has already determined salvation for
those who believe in Him. In his book, *Going for the Gold*, Joe Wall, a
missionary to Russia, states, "Because of Christ's perfect payment for sin
at the cross, the only other judgment facing the Christian is the
Judgment Seat of Christ, or the bema. The issue of our eternal salvation
has already been settled. There's no condemnation for those who are in
Christ Jesus. Our entrance into His eternal kingdom is secure, without a
doubt!"[20] Absolutely forgiven by God, we are now freely loved.

When we accept this fact as truth, we're free to love ourselves and others. For me, the most difficult person to love is *me*. The main culprit in
my failure to see myself through God's eyes is illegitimate shame. There
is legitimate shame that helps us to see ourselves as we really are and
moves us toward God; however, illegitimate shame drives us away from
God, while taking away our ability to reach outside of ourselves to show

the love of Jesus to the world. This kind of shame creates a deep inner contempt. We don't feel worthy to be loved, so we're afraid to be seen as we really are. Exposure could mean that no one would love us.

I've discovered that I can't love when I'm self-focused. Dr. Dan B. Allender, in his book *The Wounded Heart,* provides this insight about how illegitimate shame blocks our ability to love: "The dread of being found out is sufficient to fuel radical denial, workaholism, perfectionism, revictimization, and a host of other ills. But the fear is greater than simply losing relationship. It is the terror that if our dark soul is discovered, we will never be enjoyed, nor desired, nor pursued by anyone."[21] We experience shame for many reasons. My own shame is, for the most part, a result of sexual abuse. Simply stated, shame is the terror of being seen as we really are; therefore, we find it difficult to love others when shame grows its deep roots within us.

The terror of shame will evaporate at the *bema* where Christ longs to reward us for our service to Him. He loves us exactly the way we are and died for us, even though he knew about our sin. How he sees us will be observed by all at the Judgment. Paul wrote to Timothy about these rewards: "In the future there is laid up for me the crown of righteousness, which the Lord, the righteous Judge, will award to me on that day; and not only to me, but also to all who have loved His appearing" (2 Timothy 4:8). When we remember what's ahead, we can love and accept ourselves for who we are. For many of us, this will be a long and difficult process, but in the end, Christ will reward us fairly, and with love.

Unfortunately, the art of love has been lost in the evangelical church; instead, judgment seems to be the norm. In our city, there is a wonderful church full of what the world considers unlovable people: recovering addicts. Tattoos and prison experiences are commonplace. Tales of scarred lives, lost families, and struggles to stay sober are told, then complete acceptance is demonstrated. In fact, when the pastor is asked for directions, he simply says, "Go south until you see two hundred people smoking outside before the service. Then, you've found our church." These people have learned to love themselves; in turn, they can now love others.

Exponential growth is happening within this church community.

From January until September of 2006, Pastor Larry baptized over eighty new Christians. Over three hundred addicts have either received Jesus for the first time as their personal Savior or re-dedicated their lives to Him. It's truly an amazing work of the Holy Spirit, and the blessing that He offers is clear for everyone to see.

Sadly, I'm not sure that these men and women would be welcome in most churches. They don't dress like most churchgoers, and some might use foul language. Cigarette butts may fill trash cans after the service. Their presence might interrupt our sterile, perfect timing. They may get up and walk during the sermon, and some may feel the need to interact with the pastor. Also, what kind of example would a tattoo-filled church be to our children? I remember when we invited the Sober Project to become a part of our church. Pastor Larry looked at our elders and said, "I'm not sure you're ready for my people. Some of them smell bad; they're brash, and they don't talk nice." There are many times when the Church fails to love the unlovable because it's simply too inconvenient. Our lives are disrupted when truly loving others forces us out of our comfort zone. Once again, our comfort gets in the way of eternal rewards.

Jesus calls His children to love others. How we loved others will be a prerequisite for rewards at the bema. Love also enriches our lives in the here and now. C.S. Lewis, in his sermon *The Weight of Glory* said, "The load, or weight, or burden of my neighbour's glory should be laid on my back, a load so heavy that only humility can carry it, and the backs of the proud will be broken. It is a serious thing to live in a society of possible gods and goddesses, to remember that the dullest and most uninteresting person you can talk to may one day be the creature which, if you say it now, you would be strongly tempted to worship, or else a horror and a corruption such as you now meet, if at all, only in a nightmare. All day long we are, in some degree, helping each other to one or other of these destinations."[22]

Love causes the *backs of the proud to be broken*. Pride and love don't go together. There are times when I hear a conceited voice inside of me that whispers, *you are better than him*. When I subtly believe that I am better than others, however, I can't love them.

Many biblical records prove my point. Several notable men and women of the Scriptures constantly battled against pride, which blocked their ability to love those who were unlike them or a threat to their position.

Joseph's brothers are a perfect example. Their pride caused them to hate their youngest brother; any love they felt for him had been burned away in a jealous rage. In the thirty-seventh chapter of Genesis, the narrative of Joseph's life begins with a bang. Joseph's brothers were jealous of a gift he'd received from their father. Not only did Joseph receive a special coat from Jacob, but he also had unwisely shared a dream about his future rule over them. Their anger and pride led to a horrible plan. The wickedness of Joseph's brothers is clearly obvious in this account: "When they saw him from a distance, and before he came close to them, they plotted against him to put him to death. And they said to one another, 'Here comes this dreamer! Now then, come and let us kill him and throw him into one of the pits; and we will say, 'A wild beast devoured him.' Then let us see what will become of his dreams'" (Genesis 37:18-20). Only Reuben's objection of conscience saved the young boy's life. God's providence then brought Joseph to Egypt as a slave. Because of Joseph's faithfulness, he eventually became second-in-command to Pharaoh. He'd been exalted because of his humility. Reconciliation only took place when Joseph forgave their debt of sin. Humility allowed Joseph to embark on a love relationship with his errant brothers, and his love for God allowed him to keep an eternal perspective.

In chapter fifteen of Acts, we read about the Jerusalem Council, which was convened because legalistic rituals were standing in the way of love. Jewish Christians who had been circumcised believed that their Gentile brothers should follow suit. Somewhere in the hearts of these new Christians, they must have thought, *I am better than a Gentile because I am circumcised.* Their limited viewpoint didn't include an eternal mindset. The apostle Peter even joined in this hypocrisy by eating with the pro-circumcision crowd. In Galatians 2:11-13, Paul and Barnabas set the record straight, but the damage had been done. For many years afterward, the pride of circumcision created an obstacle for Jewish believers as they learned how to love the Gentiles.

Jesus' disciples also found it difficult to love others because of pride.

Families brought their children to spend time with the Lord. The disciples may have thought to themselves, *Jesus is too important to waste time with children.* Obviously, this wasn't the truth at all. Mark recorded such an incident: "And they were bringing children to Him so that He might touch them; and the disciples rebuked them. But when Jesus saw this, He was indignant and said to them, 'Permit the children to come to Me; do not hinder them; for the kingdom of God belongs to such as these'" (Mark 10:13, 14). The disciples couldn't love these children properly because of their pride. Jesus loved them with all of His heart and made an eternal point as He rebuked the disciples' temporal mindset.

Seeing life through the lens of *now* seriously compromises our ability to love ourselves and others. Many false worldly belief systems, for example, cause us to despise ourselves. We compare ourselves to others against the backdrop of the culture. We think, *I'm not pretty enough, smart enough, popular enough,* or *sinless enough to be loved.* As Christians, we add to the self-deceptions against the backdrop of the church: *I don't know the Bible well enough to participate in church activities, so I'm not as good as others.* Negative self-talk is bound to occur when we compare ourselves to others; however, God calls us to see ourselves as He sees us.

Consider what the Bible says about God's care for us. First, we are God's most treasured creation: "Are not two sparrows sold for a cent? And *yet* not one of them will fall to the ground apart from your Father. But the very hairs of your head are all numbered. Therefore do not fear; you are of more value than many sparrows" (Matthew 10:29-31).

Second, God is concerned about every aspect of our lives: "Every good thing given and every perfect gift is from above, coming down from the Father of lights, with whom there is no variation or shifting shadow" (James 1:17). The author of Hebrews used portions from the books of Deuteronomy, Joshua, and Psalms to write: "Make sure that your character is free from the love of money, being content with what you have; for He Himself has said, "I WILL NEVER DESERT YOU NOR WILL I EVER FORSAKE YOU," so that we may confidently say, 'THE LORD IS MY HELPER. I WILL NOT BE AFRAID. WHAT SHALL MAN DO TO ME?'" (Hebrews 13:5, 6).

Third, when we walk in His will, the Lord desires to lavish Himself on us: "Ask and it shall be given to you; seek, and you shall find; knock and it shall be opened to you. For everyone who asks receives, and he who seeks finds, and to him who knocks it shall be opened. Or what man is there among you who, when his son shall ask him for a loaf, will give him a stone? Or if he shall ask for a fish, he will not give him a snake, will he? If you then, being evil, know how to give good gifts to your children, how much more shall your Father who is in heaven give what is good to those who ask Him!'" (Matthew 7:7-11).

Fourth, God shepherds us. He desires to reward us for obedience: "The Lord is my shepherd, I shall not want. He makes me lie down in green pastures; He leads me beside quiet waters. He restores my soul; He guides me in the paths of righteousness for His name's sake. Even though I walk through the valley of the shadow of death, I fear no evil, for You art with me; Your rod and Your staff, they comfort me. You prepare a table before me in the presence of my enemies; You have anointed my head with oil; my cup overflows. Surely goodness and lovingkindness will follow me all the days of my life, and I will dwell in the house of the Lord forever" (Psalm 23).

Love is the centerpiece of the gospel message. Biblical evidence clearly shows that God loves you, and you can love yourself too. When you learn to love yourself the way Christ loves you, you'll be free to love others.

Of course, theological knowledge, Scripture memorization, service to the body of Christ, and spiritual growth are all essential for grasping the big picture of God. We gain truth when we embark on these pathways, but we can live in error if we take one of these aspects away from our spiritual journey.

Love, however, is the central part of the person of Christ. Anticipation of the *bema* causes us to examine how well we love others. Joe Wall lists "Ten Principles of Wise Spiritual Investments" in his marvelous book entitled *Going for the Gold.* These are godly standards to build on as we prepare ourselves to meet Christ. Notice how many of them involve love and ministry toward others:

1. *Invest in the lives of those who minister the Word...* "The one who is taught the word is to share all good things with the one who teaches

him. Do not be deceived, God is not mocked; for whatever a man sows, this he will also reap" (Galatians 6:6,7).

2. *Minister to those in need...* "And whoever in the name of a disciple gives to one of these little ones even a cup of cold water to drink, truly I say to you, he shall not lose his reward" (Matthew 10:42).

3. *Sacrifice to follow Christ...* "Then Peter said to Him, 'Behold, we have left everything and followed You; what then will there be for us?' And Jesus said to them, 'Truly I say to you, that you who have followed Me, in the regeneration when the Son of Man will sit on His glorious throne, you also shall sit upon twelve thrones, judging the twelve tribes of Israel. And everyone who has left houses or brothers or sisters or father or mother or children or farms for My name's sake, shall receive many times as much, and shall inherit eternal life. But many who are first will be last; and *the* last, first'" (Matthew 19:27-29).

4. *Give without fanfare...* "Beware of practicing your righteousness before men to be noticed by them; otherwise you have no reward with your Father who is in heaven" (Matthew 6:1).

5. *Accept abuse for the sake of Christ...* "Blessed are you when people insult you and persecute you, and falsely say all kinds of evil against you because of Me. 'Rejoice and be glad, for your reward in heaven is great; for in the same way they persecuted the prophets who were before you'" (Matthew 5:11, 12).

6. *Pray in secret...* "When you pray, you are not to be like the hypocrites; for they love to stand and pray in the synagogues and on the street corners so that they may be seen by men. Truly I say to you, they have their reward in full. But you, when you pray, go into your inner room, close your door and pray to your Father who is in secret, and your Father who sees what is done in secret will reward you" (Matthew 6:5, 6).

7. *Engage in spiritual activity without fanfare...* "Whenever you fast, do not put on a gloomy face as the hypocrites do, for they neglect their appearance so that they will be noticed by men when they are fasting. Truly, I say to you, they have their reward in full. But you, when you fast, anoint your head and wash your face so that your fasting will not be noticed by men, but by your Father who is in secret; and your

Father who sees what is done in secret will reward you" (Matthew 6:16-18).

8. *Love your enemies by being willing to help them...* "But love your enemies, and do good, and lend, expecting nothing in return; and your reward will be great..." (Luke 6:35a).

9. *Give hearty service to the Lord and not just to please men...* "Whatever you do, do your work heartily, as for the Lord rather than for men, knowing that from the Lord you will receive the reward of the inheritance. It is the Lord Christ whom you serve" (Colossians 3:23, 24).

10. *Entertain those who cannot repay you...* "And He also went on to say to the one who had invited Him, 'When you give a luncheon or a dinner, do not invite your friends or your brothers or your relatives or rich neighbors, otherwise they may also invite you in return and that will be your repayment. But when you give a reception, invite the poor, the crippled, the lame, the blind, and you will be blessed, since they do not have the means to repay you; for you will be repaid at the resurrection of the righteous" (Luke 14:12-14).

In summary, Walls states, "We spend too much of our time planning the purchase of houses, cars, electronic gadgets, and setting up our investment portfolios. We would be wiser to focus our attention on investing in the lives of others and serving the Lord more effectively."[23]

Remember, Paul tells us in 1 Corinthians 13:13 that love is the greatest virtue we can pursue. When we love others, we're most like Christ. Rewards await us at the *bema* when lives are changed. By loving others, we'll attract them to Jesus. We "trade up" when we learn to love ourselves and others.

—

Jake looked around at the men in the room. The atmosphere reminded him of the many other government agencies he'd visited. He had been in and out of psychiatric hospitals because of his battle against depression and suicidal actions. He'd seen his share of counselors and wondered if this group would be any different.

This was a therapy group made up of sexual abuse victims. There were two facilitators and eight men of different ages, colors, and sexual orientation gathered in a circle. The men had one main thing in common: they were all victims of abuse. Jake wondered if he could overcome his past.

As a young man, Jake lived with his grandparents in a small northeastern town because his parents had divorced when he was only eight years old. His mother died two years later, and his dad was an alcoholic. His earliest memories of his father still haunted him. Each Saturday, his father arranged things so the two of them could be alone. He was led to a field, where he was abused there every weekend for five years. The abuse didn't stop until he was old enough to fight back.

Jake hated his father who had abused him, along with his mother, who abandoned him by dying, and his grandparents, who had ignored the abuse. He hated himself more. The words, *I could have stopped it,* ran through his head. Every day, he asked himself, *how could I have been so stupid?*

High school was a nightmare for Jake. He related to men through sex because he didn't know how to do it any other way. His classmates accused him of being a homosexual and harassed him daily. He liked girls, but he had no idea how to talk to them. Because of his background of sexual abuse, he felt trapped.

Throughout college and young adulthood, Jake's destructive patterns continued. He became involved in numerous relationships with other men. Overwhelmed by emptiness, he tried suicide for the first time. It would be the first of many attempts to end his life. For Jake, life was unbearable.

As he sat and listened to the men in his group tell their stories, Jake's mind went back to a meeting he attended in college. The group was called *Campus ...something or other... for Christ.* One of the guys in his dorm had invited him to come. He still had vivid memories of that evening. About thirty students packed into a dorm lounge were singing songs he didn't know, and they used a lot of words that he didn't understand. But there was something real there. As weird as this group was, *at least they believed in something,* he thought.

The student who spoke said things that Jake had never heard before.

He said that someone's old life could pass away, and a new life could start. Jake thought, *if they only knew…*

The meeting ended, and Jake walked back to his room with the man who had invited him. Jake remembered that he was asked, *what'd you think? Do you want to start over…your life I mean? Do you want to accept Jesus as your personal Savior?* He felt a stirring of hope within his soul as he remembered what happened next. The student showed him Bible verses that explained why Jesus came to earth. Jake learned that his sins could be forgiven, so he accepted Jesus that night. The next two weeks were an intense whirlwind of Bible study and prayer. He learned more about his new relationship with Christ. For the first time in his life, he began to experience joy.

Unfortunately, the dorm emptied out at Christmas break, and Jake went home to stay with his grandparents. The graves of his parents seemed to call to him as he drove by and brought him back to reality. His life-giving experiences at school seemed like a passing dream. The next four weeks were like hell.

The banker called and said there wasn't enough money for his grandparents to keep the house, so Jake went back to work. He never saw those college students again and ended up back in his hometown. Now, he sat in another support group as the tragic stories of abuse droned on and on.

Jake's quest for temporal satisfaction took on these forms:

- His willingness to be a victim
- His willingness to let his past define him
- His unwillingness to pursue a Christian faith that had begun to bear fruit
- His unwillingness to love himself.

Jake's hatred for himself and others derailed his quest for eternal treasure. He has made a decision to follow Jesus, so he'll be in heaven someday. God has provided a group that could help him, but he's only going through the motions. Because he's never learned to love himself, Jake will have a hard time loving others. His only hope is to rediscover an intimate relationship with Christ. To help him do that, he can contact his Christian friends from college. He still has the resources needed to study the Bible and knows where the neighborhood church is located, but he'll have to make the final decision.

—

Lisa put a circle around the important words that she noticed in her study of Ephesians 4. She especially enjoyed today's study on verses 17-19: "So this I say, and affirm together with the Lord, that you walk no longer just as the Gentiles also walk, in the futility of their mind, being darkened in their understanding, excluded from the life of God because of the ignorance that is in them, because of the hardness of their heart; and they, having become callous, have given themselves over to sensuality, for the practice of every kind of impurity with greediness."

Boy, that's true, Lisa thought to herself as she closed her Bible and placed her pen inside the cover. *This world is full of people like that.* The leader handed out homework, and then Lisa was on her way to a lunch appointment with a group of mothers from her son's school. The subject matter would be *creationism.* She felt tightness in her chest when she remembered that one of the women wasn't on her side. *How could any Christian not want creationism taught in schools?* Well, she'd control her anger. The other woman was outnumbered, so Lisa was sure to get her way.

The restaurant was one of Lisa's favorites. She was glad when she noticed that the two women sitting at a table in the back were the ones who agreed with her. This would give them a chance to plan an effective strategy.

This was an important luncheon. The school board would rely heavily upon the recommendation from this committee. Unfortunately, the issue had become divisive. Religious groups were pitted against non-religious ones, and at times, the rhetoric had gotten nasty. The ladies quickly planned their strategy before the other woman joined the group.

After getting the small talk out of the way, the group got down to business. There were three women who ardently wanted the school system to teach *creationism* in the classroom. Lisa was an evangelical, but the other two didn't attend church. The woman opposed to the proposal was also a Christian who attended a strong Bible-teaching church.

Each woman expressed their opinion, and now it came time for the moment of truth. Lisa trembled when she turned to her opponent and said, "Okay, tell us why you feel like evolution is so important to our children, but teaching about God isn't?" The question produced immediate tension in the air, but the woman answered with cool professionalism.

"Lisa, it's not fair to say that I want evolution to be taught in our schools. I don't believe in evolution. I believe that God created all things, but I also believe that parents are responsible to teach their children about God. If we allow creationism to become a part of the school's curriculum, then parents will have one more excuse to let someone else mentor their children. Many parents, at least at our church, already think that the youth pastor is responsible for their kids. If we teach this in school, then it's one more reason to leave our kids alone. Besides, evolution is so ridiculous, that if a parent simply talks through the issue with the child, it really becomes a non-issue."

"That's it?" Lisa replied.

"That's it."

"You do realize that when we vote, everyone will know that you voted against us?"

"Yes."

Lisa decided it was time to wrap things up. "Well, let's vote then. I just hope you can live with yourself. I wonder what your pastor teaches. No wonder your church is so large. You probably have Darwin's books in the library." Lisa knew that she had gone too far, but it was too late. The words were already blurted out. Her emotion had gotten the best of her. *At least, creationism would be taught in her son's school.* That was plenty of consolation in itself.

"No," the woman replied as tears formed in her eyes. "No, we love the Lord. I think I'd better go. You know how I feel." With those words, a devastated woman left the restaurant.

Lisa had done major spiritual damage by wounding another Christian's spirit and being a poor witness in front of her non-Christian committee members. With her critical words, she managed to drive a wedge between good churches.

Lisa's quest for temporal satisfaction took on these forms:

- Her head knowledge of the Bible that doesn't connect with her actions
- Her failure to value the relationship of another Christian over an issue, even a vitally important issue such as creation vs. evolution
- Her unwillingness to hear another viewpoint, even one she didn't agree with, because of her self-righteousness
- Her inability to love others because of her desire to be right.

Neither Jake nor Lisa have "traded up." Jake can't love himself, and Lisa doesn't love others. Sadly, though they both have resources to change their behavior, neither one seems willing to move out of a self-imposed comfort zone that takes away eternal rewards.

What about you? You can begin to love yourself and others when you answer these questions:

1. Why do you study the Bible? Do you study for the sake of knowledge or do you study to become like Christ?
2. Do you feel the need to be right?
3. Are you willing to sacrifice relationships in order to be right?
4. Are there things in your past that you haven't dealt with?
5. Does your self-hatred result in anger that is directed toward others and God?
6. Will you walk in pain in order to heal?
7. Do you see yourself as a victim?
8. Do you like to play the victim?
9. Does your victim mentality take away your responsibility to love yourself and others?
10. On a scale of one to ten, how important is it for you to love others?

Notes:

_____

_____

_____

_____

_____

_____

_____

Prayer to Love Myself and Others:

Father, Your Son loved others. He put His own needs aside because of love. He even allowed Himself to die because of love. I want to be like Him. Teach me to love others the way You love them. Also, teach me to love myself. Help me to learn to see myself the way You see me. Never let me forget the price that was paid for me. Let me love myself because You love me. Then, I will be free to love others and make an impact for Your kingdom. Amen.

> *"A new commandment I give to you, that you love one another,*
> *even as I have loved you, that you also love one another.*
> *By this all men will know that you are My disciples,*
> *if you have love for one another."*
>
> John 13: 34, 35

18. Zane C. Hodges, *Absolutely Free: A Biblical Reply to Lordship Salvation* (Grand Rapids: Zondervan, 1989), 150.
19. *The Catholic Encyclopedia, Volume VII* (Robert Appleton Company, 1910).
20. Joe Wall, *Going for the Gold* (Houston: Xulon Press, 2005) 33-34.
21. Dr. Dan B. Allender, *The Wounded Heart: Hope for Adult Victims of Childhood Sexual Abuse* (Colorado Springs: NavPress, 1990), 71.
22. C.S. Lewis, *The Weight of Glory* (Grand Rapids: Eerdmans, 1977), 14-15.
23. Wall, *Going for the Gold*, 115-120.

7   When I *Trade Up* I Can Have Joy that Lasts!

We are building up to a crescendo: the final two chapters emphasize the point of this book. When we trade temporal satisfaction for eternal treasure, we find joy. While we pursue the world's goods, that kind of joy escapes us, and we'll also lose precious rewards at the *bema*.

A few minutes ago, as I was writing, a friend called me. He's suffering because his wife has filed for divorce, but he desperately wants to save his marriage. Daily, he struggles to keep his faith. He said, "Paul, I know that God is in control. I have prayed that the Lord would achieve His purposes through this event. Yet, I still feel a huge hole in my gut. Does that mean that I don't have faith? Why can't I find joy?"

I explained to him that having faith doesn't mean there won't be pain. God grieves because of divorce. No matter how bad the circumstances are, however, we can still experience joy that lasts when we understand there's Someone at work behind the scenes whom we can't see. Our joy is in God and all of what makes Him God. When situations turn against us, true joy does not waver.

Americans seem desperate for joy. Our culture spotlights this quest through mass-media campaigns, while societal values change with every whim. Joy is the goal, but the end now justifies the means.

Evangelical church leaders have exploited this quest for joy. The gospel message of sacrifice and self-denial has virtually disappeared from our nation's pulpits. All that's left is a hollow doctrine that leaves a permanent solution by the wayside. The pursuit of Christ has been whittled down to an indefinable, obscure quest to love Him. This is a good goal, but it's not adequate in itself. Following Jesus does not necessarily bring happiness into the life of the believer; instead, the opposite may be true. When we accept Jesus as our Savior, we may experience more pain and greater trials. He never promised that this life would make us giddy, but He did guarantee us a deeper and more mature sense of well-being, which brings true joy that lasts. The pursuit of instant gratification, however, can overshadow our quest for joy.

The Standard College Dictionary defines joy as "1. a strong feeling of happiness arising from the expectation of some good, or from its realization; gladness; delight. 2. *a state of contentment or satisfaction: to have delight.*"[24] The second meaning perfectly defines biblical faith.

Joy is inspired by a right relationship to God. In fact, *all things* that are related to God bring joy, even judgment (1 Chronicles 16:33) and faithfulness in times of trouble (Job 6:10). Joy is not found in the *absence* of trials, but in the faithfulness of God *through* trials.

The biblical references to joy also include wonderful things. Joy comes from personal victory (Psalm 21:1), one's ability to give a right reply (Proverbs 15:23), material blessings (Jeremiah 31:12), the birth of a baby (John 16:21), physical healing (Acts 8:8), cheerful looks (Proverbs 15:30), enjoyment of good food and drink (Ecclesiastes 8:15), and a joyful reveling in the company of friends and family (Philippians 1:26; 2 Timothy 1:4; 2 John 12). Joy is a part of everyday life that's based on God and consists of long-term contentment. God gives us joy that's an abiding inner sense of well-being, but how much we experience it depends on our relationship with Him.

In his personal biography entitled, *Retrospect,* the great missionary, James Hudson Taylor, defines joy in this way: "It is the consciousness of the threefold joy of the Lord: His joy in ransoming us, His joy in dwelling within us as our Saviour and Power for fruitbearing and His joy in possessing us, as His Bride and His delight; it is the consciousness of this joy which is our real strength. Our joy in Him may be a fluctuating thing: His joy in us knows no change." Notice that this definition of joy is solely based on the person of God, which doesn't change.

St. Augustine, one of history's greatest theologians, was quoted in the enlightening *Ethics of St. Augustine*: "There is a joy which is not given to the ungodly, but to those who love Thee for Thine own sake, whose joy Thou Thyself art. And this is the happy life, to rejoice to Thee, of Thee, for Thee; this it is, and there is no other." For Augustine, God is the center of all joy.

This anonymous quote sums up the matter perfectly: "Happiness depends on happenings; joy depends on Christ." When *happenings* turn against us, the Lord is still the same.

It's good to pursue happiness because God gave us certain things to make us happy. Moreover, Jesus came to give us abundant life (John 10:10). God wants us to enjoy our spouses, children, homes, friends, nature, recreation, and other activities in the *here and now*; however, a problem arises when the pursuit of temporal happiness outweighs the quest for eternal treasure.

Jesus used a parable to make this point: "The land of a rich man was very productive. And he began reasoning to himself, saying, 'What shall I do, since I have no place to store my crops?' Then he said, 'This is what I will do: I will tear down my barns and build larger ones, and there I will store all my grain and my goods. And I will say to my soul, "Soul, you have many goods laid up for many years to come; take your ease, eat, drink and be merry.' But God said to him, 'You fool! This very night your soul is required of you; and now who will own what you have prepared?' So is the man who stores up treasure for himself, and is not rich toward God" (Luke 12:16-21). Jesus couldn't have laid it out more clearly. It isn't important to pursue worldly satisfaction, because that will only lead to filling barns with meaningless objects and relationships, leaving us with nothing to offer at the *bema*. But we can be *rich toward God*. This wonderful phrase reminds us that rewards await us when we're rich in Him. In other words, God desires to give us all of Himself.

When I fill my barn with worldly and temporal things, there is no room for God. I may gain a false sense of security by relying on the things that fill my barn rather than on God. This is an easy trap to fall into.

After a wealthy young man had rejected His offer of joy, Jesus said to His disciples, "Truly I say to you, it is hard for a rich man to enter the kingdom of heaven" (Matthew 19:23). Once we have gained worldly things, it's hard to give them up because we tend to worship our possessions. How can God find a place in which to fill our soul when it's already full of junk? The earthly hay in our barn will only burn away in the end. For some, this means that nearly the entire building will be destroyed. In your barn, how much room is available for eternal possessions?

Worldly possessions that look good and seem to fill us are intoxicating; meanwhile, however, they kill our souls. Jesus reminded the rich man, "… *your soul will be required of you.*" Are we planning for the future, or is the temporary joy of the world causing us to forget that a moment of reckoning will come?

I once worked for a very rich, well-known man who was the owner of a National Football League Team, as well as a professional soccer team. He even had a stadium named after him. His million-dollar lifestyle was envied. He flew in a private jet, and his family stayed in the finest hotels. Tragically, only worldly objects filled his barn.

As I watched this man, I didn't observe any joy in his life. All he experienced was pain from family squabbles. After his death, the people closest to him fought over his estate. His name was removed from the stadium which he'd built, and his sports empire fell apart. He was like the man in 1 Corinthians 3 whose work resulted in wood, hay, and straw that burned away. Only God knows if this man *escaped as through fire,* but there's little doubt that his earthly possessions didn't give him lasting joy.

It's essential that you keep your eyes fixed on eternity. Satan will continue to throw the world's treasures at your feet. They'll always look good, and some will be almost impossible to reject, especially when everyone tells you to embrace them. In order to discern the helpful from the harmful, it may come down to just between you and God.

This leads us back to the most important element of "trading up": we must develop an intimate relationship with God. The Lord has promised that He'll help us discern what's best for us.

First, we can take joy in knowing that nothing will come our way that can't be handled by Him. Paul reminded the Corinthian church of this truth: "No temptation has overtaken you but such as is common to man; and God is faithful, who will not allow you to be tempted beyond what you are able, but with the temptation will provide the way of escape also, so that you will be able to endure it" (1 Corinthians 10:13). No temptation is too powerful for us to handle when Christ is at our side.

Second, we can have confidence that an intimate relationship with the Lord will allow the Holy Spirit to speak to us in words we can understand: "Your ears will hear a word behind you, 'This is the way, walk in it,' whenever you turn to the right or to the left" (Isaiah 30:21). An increasing intimacy with Christ will help us distinguish between what is good and what is better.

Third, a vital relationship with Jesus will also help us to correctly interpret the Bible (the most reliable way of interpreting God's messages to us), and choose friends that can give us proper counsel. While we're involved in an intimate relationship with God, we're protected by His wisdom and power. On the other hand, when we stray outside of His umbrella, we're on our own, and Satan will move in for the kill. If we forsake our relationship with Jesus, we'll lose our joy.

Lasting joy comes only through a genuine relationship with Christ in which we learn to cherish eternal treasures while discarding temporal things. When we embrace intimacy with Christ, we "trade up." The process of finding lasting joy has begun.

Unfortunately, not all believers are willing to "trade up." John Piper asks, "Is this experience of the love of God the same for all believers? No, not in degree. If all believers had the same experience of the love of God, Paul would not have prayed for the Ephesians that they 'be able to comprehend with all the saints what is the breadth and length and height and depth, and to know the love of Christ which surpasses knowledge' (Ephesians 3:18, 19). He prayed this because some were deficient in their experience of this love of God in Christ. How then do we pursue the fullness of the experience of the love of God poured out in our hearts by the Holy Spirit? One key is to realize that the experience is not like hypnosis or electric shock or drug-induced hallucinations or shivers at a good tune. Rather it is mediated through knowledge. It is not the same as knowledge. But it comes through knowledge. Or to say it another way, this experience of the love of God is the work of the Spirit giving unspeakable joy in response to the mind's perception of the demonstration of that love in Jesus Christ. In this way Christ gets the glory for the joy that we have. It is a joy in what we see in him."[25] Piper rightly states that lasting joy comes from Christ. It takes effort to achieve this kind of joy, and not every Christian is willing to do that. The ones who do, "trade up." They find themselves enmeshed in the person of Christ, who gives lasting joy.

The Bible is full of verses that support this concept. Piper continues, "In fact, 1 Peter 1:6 says that the joy itself is 'in' the truth that Peter is telling us about the work of Christ. It says, "In this you greatly rejoice." And what is 'this'? It is the truth that 1) in "His great mercy [God] has caused us to be born again to a living hope through the resurrection of Jesus Christ from the dead"; 2) we will "obtain an inheritance which is imperishable and undefiled and will not fade away;" and 3) we "are protected by the power of God through faith for a salvation ready to be revealed in the last time" (1 Peter 1:3-5). In this we "greatly rejoice with joy inexpressible and full of glory." We know something. In this we rejoice! The experience of unspeakable joy is a mediated experience. It comes through knowledge of Christ and His work. It has content. Consider also Galatians 3:5: "Does He who provides you with the Spirit and works miracles among you do it by the works of the Law, or by hearing with faith?" We know from Romans 5:5 that the experience of the love of God is "through the Holy Spirit who is given to us." But now Galatians 3:5 tells us that this supply of the Spirit is not without content. It is "by hearing with faith." Two things: hearing and faith. There is the hearing of the truth about Christ, and there is the faith in that truth. This is how the Spirit is supplied. He comes through knowing and believing. His work is a mediated work. It has mental content. Beware of seeking the Spirit by emptying your head. Similarly, Romans 15:13 says that the God of hope fills us with joy and peace "in believing." And believing has content. The love of God is experienced in knowing and believing Christ because, as Romans 8:39 says the love of God is "in Christ Jesus our Lord." Nothing will be able to separate us "from the love of God, which is in Christ Jesus our Lord."[26] The inheritance referred to in 1 Peter

1:6 is eternal treasure. By meeting and knowing Christ, we can obtain that treasure. Intimacy with Christ comes when we read the Bible, pray often, listen to affirming words through music and Bible teaching, and submit ourselves to Jesus.

Spiritual disciplines allow us to become better at doing things. The most difficult of these is submission, an act of the will that can be extremely costly. We'll quickly find out how much we love God by the measure of our submission to Him. He will ask us to venture into a place where we have no control; there, we'll find Him. It's not until we've lost ourselves that we can find Christ. Then, the divine inheritance can be ours, and "trading up" is possible.

Finding Christ at the end of ourselves changes the way we live because our bondage to self is now broken. We no longer live to please others, satisfy longings, worry about the future, wonder what God thinks of us, or earn His favor. Now, we are free to define our legacy, live in victory, stop wasting time, love ourselves, and find lasting joy.

These are the life-maximizing benefits of trading temporal satisfaction for eternal treasure. Giving all of ourselves to Christ is the key to "trading up" and the only way to find lasting joy.

If you aren't willing to travel this path, then you'll end up mired in discouragement and missing all that God has for you. But you don't have to live like that. God can be like a giant tow-truck that can hoist you out of the mud. Then, He can completely cleanse you so that you can start over. He's waiting for you right now. Why wait any longer?

—

Lambert Dolphin challenges all of us with these life-changing words: "Many people think that the mark of an authentic Christian is doctrinal purity; if a person's beliefs are biblical and doctrinally orthodox, then he is a Christian. People who equate orthodoxy with authenticity find it hard to even consider the possibility that, despite the correctness of all their doctrinal positions, they may have missed the deepest reality of the authentic Christian life. But we must never forget that true Christianity is more than teaching—it is a way of life. In fact, it is life itself. 'He who has the Son has life,' remember? When we talk about life, we are talking about something that is far more than mere morality, far more than doctrinal accuracy."[27] Is Christ your life? Make Him so and then you can trade up. You'll maximize your life both now and for all eternity. You can reign with Christ.

—

Ann was everyone's favorite woman. She was a spark plug who did everything well. The people at her church adored her because she was young, pretty, and full of enthusiasm. Everyone knew that if a job needed to be done right, Ann was your girl.

The church Ann attended was small by today's standards. There were about two hundred people in the congregation and two staff members. The pastors regularly found themselves stretched to the limit, so Ann was the first person they'd call. They knew Ann would always say yes.

Today was no exception. The Children's Director was down with the flu. Ann had received an early phone call, and even though she wasn't feeling well herself, she dragged herself to church. Her job this morning was to check children into their Sunday school rooms. As usual, Ann's smile made everyone feel like a million dollars. She had fulfilled her duty; the pastor called and she had said yes. *That's what Christians do,* she thought.

She was tired. It was the afternoon and her three children, all under five years old, were screaming for something to eat. Ann wanted to grab a bite at the nearest fast-food restaurant, but her budget was tight. Instead, she drove home and prepared lunch for her entire family. By 2 p.m., Ann was exhausted, but her day wasn't over yet. AWANA started at 4 p.m.

Ann attempted to put the kids down for a quick nap, but they just weren't in the mood. She knew that her husband would be home soon, and he'd be hungry, as he always was after a day of golf. By the time she was finished making the meatloaf and re-dressing the kids, it was time to leave. Her husband hadn't come home, so she would catch up with him later.

Back at the church, Ann resumed her normal duties of a *cubbies* leader. She dutifully ran between rooms, making sure that all of her leaders had been taken care of. She didn't particularly like this kind of position. To tell the truth, she would rather be involved with the music ministry, since she was an excellent guitarist, having learned to play. She often led group singing times, but, unfortunately, her time and energy were needed elsewhere. Because she believed "this is what Christians do," she filled whatever position she could.

When Ann came home, her husband was holding a meatloaf sandwich in one hand and a television remote in the other. There was a football game on, so she was glad to get at least a nod from him. She wished that he'd be more involved with her and the kids at church, but she also realized that Jack wasn't a Christian.

They'd met seven years ago at a nightclub. The physical attraction between them was overwhelming, so they were married within a year. The first two years of the marriage were difficult for her because Jack didn't meet Ann's longing for emotional intimacy. He rather seemed more concerned with stock prices and sports scores. She did what she could to please him, and the marriage somehow survived.

Two years later, the first of three children entered their lives. She hoped that Jack would change. He did for a short while, but then he was back to normal. She took care of the baby and Jack, while he only took care of himself.

She couldn't discuss these issues with him. Whenever she would hint that she wanted more in their marriage, Jack would remind her that he was a good provider. He did take care of her by earning a six-figure income. All of their physical needs were met, but emotionally, Ann was dying. Her heart was closing up as she withdrew into herself.

During her second pregnancy, Ann met a friend at her scrap-booking club that took a special interest in her. Janice invited her to lunch, and the two went shopping together. She often shared with Ann about her relationship with Jesus, but didn't force the issue because it was just a natural part of her. After a few weeks, Janice invited Ann to a luncheon at the church, and she liked what she saw. These women seemed so full of joy and hope; they had something that Ann wanted.

In the car, Janice explained that these women knew Jesus and then led Ann in a prayer to accept Jesus as her personal Savior. It was a wonderful moment. She now had new hope that her life could change. Ann began to attend church regularly and joined numerous Bible studies. She felt her relationship with Christ begin to deepen. Just a few weeks later, life caught up with her.

Ann's childhood wasn't perfect, but she had learned to cope. She grew up in a suburb just south of Dallas. Her father worked hard, but wasn't home much, so she was raised by her mother. Her two older brothers left home in their late teens. This left Ann and her mother to pacify her father.

When he was home, he was quietly demanding. He liked routine: if Ann's mother failed to have dinner ready for him, he wouldn't talk to her for a long time. The two ladies learned to tip-toe around his emotions. As the center of the home, he paid the bills and that was that. For Ann, pleasing father became a daily goal.

Ann had sworn to herself that she would marry a different kind of a man. Sadly, Jack was much like her father— a good worker, but emotionally non-existent. She found herself trying to please him, spending each day making sure that Jack wouldn't get into one of his moods, thereby protecting the children from him. Deep down within her soul, she wanted him to love her, but she ended up settling for his paycheck.

People-pleasing was bred into Ann from an early age. Pleasing others helped her avoid conflict, which was bad. Someone always got hurt when there was an argument, and the emotional tension drained her energy. So, she'd do whatever it took to keep away from conflict. If Jack didn't think she was important, she would draw her self-esteem from people at the church instead. Ann felt trapped.

It was getting late on that particular Sunday. As Jack watched football, Ann got the kids ready for bed. She prayed with the oldest two of her precious children, and then prayed for her baby. This was the sweetest moment of her day, when all was quiet. For just a short moment, Ann could feel the presence of God in her life. Her quiet time with the Lord was also another way to avoid Jack, but she quickly put that thought off to the side.

The kids fell asleep. Ann went to the living room and walked past Jack's chair, managing to get a grunt from him as she touched his shoulder. She sneaked off to the bedroom and turned on the television. Quietly, she opened the drawer in her bedside table and took out a glass and a bottle of wine. She would drink herself to sleep, as she did every night.

Ann's quest for temporal satisfaction took on these forms:

- Her desperate attempt to seek the praise of others
- Her persistent attempt to fill her emptiness with their praise
- Her failure to be real in front of people at her church: no one could help her because they thought she was okay
- Her unwillingness to say no, which caused her to always be busy: she didn't have time for her own personal growth
- Her failure to continue to pursue an intimate relationship with Christ
- Her failure to confront her husband on the awful state of their marriage
- Her fear of Jack's reactions
- Her continued effort to drink, quite literally, from dry wells.

Ann's plight is shared by many of us who are having a difficult time finding real joy. We smile on the outside while we're dying on the inside. We're afraid that someone might reject us if we're honest. Instead of calling on the Lord to fill us, we expect others to do so, and we're left disappointed. Human beings, however, are not designed to do what only God can do. He *alone* is the source of living water.

Satan also lies to us that confrontation is always bad, which just isn't true. When we avoid confrontation, we live in fear. By confronting each other in love, God can change our relationships (Proverbs 9:8).

Ann traded away lasting joy when she decided to please everyone. Her relationship with Christ crumbled, her self-esteem took a beating, and she suffered a loss of eternal rewards.

—

Bill was a star at work. In his two years at Techworks, he'd quickly climbed the corporate ladder. There were whispers that a VP title might soon be written next to his name.

It was time for the staff meeting, so Bill breezed into the room and took his seat. He was a few minutes late, but it didn't matter. Bill could do no wrong in anyone's eyes because he was the star. He always enjoyed the nods of affirmation when everyone liked one of his ideas and soaked in the smiles when one of his inside jokes hit the spot. This is where he was meant to be. Bill experienced what he thought was joy at Techworks.

A few months after Bill was hired, he found himself working longer hours. He told himself that he had to be there, rationalizing that the company needed him. The truth was that Bill needed the *company* because it was there he found acceptance. He also lived for the rush he received from finishing a project. The thought of going home to an empty house made him nauseated.

It was 9:30 p.m. His boss had demanded that he go home and get some sleep. Bill pulled his 2006 Lexus into his narrow driveway, just missing the old basketball hoop that he had erected there two years before. After picking up two non-descript newspapers off of his driveway, he entered the living room. Not much had changed since Sue and the kids had gone. Children's books remained neatly organized on a white shelf, with a mix of board games stacked underneath. Even Kyle's basketball still sat behind the leather armchair. Bill didn't have the heart to move it.

The upstairs bedrooms also were quietly undisturbed. The two children's rooms remained intact for the rare visit, and he didn't have the time to redecorate the master bedroom. He wasn't sure if time was the problem. Perhaps he didn't want to erase the memories. Suddenly feeling a dull ache within because of the emptiness in the house, he hurried to the television to get rid of the quietness.

Bill and Sue were married for three years before the trouble started. At first, Sue admired Bill's drive, appreciating the fact that he was willing to work to provide for their growing family. Kyle was already here, and Emily was on the way. Even though Bill worked long hours, money was never a problem.

Sue could usually convince Bill to take a few days off. She was happy to settle for Sundays, and sometimes, as a bonus, she got half of a

Saturday to be with him. On Sunday, the family went to church together. Sue and Bill often held hands as they sang worship songs. They would talk about the message on their way to lunch. Sue treasured these moments, but unfortunately, they wouldn't last.

Sue began to notice a change in Bill. He was spending less time at home because his office hours were increasing. When he *was* home, he emotionally disappeared. His mind was always on work-related things. He started to first lose interest in the kids, and then her. They talked less frequently, and eventually, their sexual relationship suffered. Soon, Bill was working on Sundays, and Sue bore the burden of hauling the kids to church. She often tried to talk to him about the message, but he wasn't listening.

Finally, on a Sunday afternoon, Sue asked Bill if he would consider starting marriage counseling. After pouring out her heart to him, she was ecstatic when he said yes. The first couple of sessions went well, and Bill appeared to be responding. He became more talkative at home, and they went to church together. But when the counselor began to focus on *his* problems, Bill decided that the counselor wasn't qualified and told Sue that he wasn't going back. Instead of changing for the better, he just worked longer hours. Their marriage deteriorated, and the abuse began.

It wasn't physical at first. He would say a harsh word to the kids or to Sue. One night, he came home and screamed at Kyle for leaving his bicycle in the driveway. It wasn't a normal voice that was just frustrated by the situation. His tone sounded so hateful that it scared Kyle and Sue. She talked to Bill about it, and he apologized. It happened again, but this time it was more intense. Sue would never forget what happened on the following evening.

It was late, and the children were in bed. Exhausted, Sue was trying to fall asleep. She heard Bill open the door, put down his keys, and head up the stairway. *I'm glad it's late,* she thought. *At least I won't need to talk with him.* She pretended to sleep, but Bill began the conversation. "Sue, look at this."

"Look at what?" she replied with her eyes half-opened.

"This is a bill from the electric company. It says that it's overdue. I work from morning until night to make sure that you have all of this."

Bill turned and made a gesture with his hands. "Now, you can't even pay the bills."

"I'm sorry," Sue said. She began to get out of bed. His anger was scaring her.

"Sorry? All you can say is sorry? That's not good enough. It's time I showed you who's boss around here." Bill came around the bed and grabbed Sue.

"No!" she screamed. "Let me go. Get your hands off of me!"

That's when Bill hit her—hard. She fell to the bed, bleeding and sobbing. He looked at his blood-stained hands and then toward the doorway. Kyle and Emily had seen the whole thing.

Sue and the kids moved out the next day, even though they were technically still married. Sue realized that God hates divorce, but she couldn't begin the process of reconciliation until he was willing to start counseling.

Bill would have to move that basketball hoop because it brought back too many sad memories. After turning on ESPN, he mulled over a project at work. *At least someone appreciates me there,* he thought.

Bill's quest for temporal satisfaction took on these forms:

- His willingness to seek to the adoration of co-workers
- His failure to realize that his low self-esteem caused him to work long hours
- His unwillingness to face the fact that joy found at the workplace would not last: he had to work longer and longer hours to earn that joy
- His unwise decision to work on Sundays rather than honor a special day with God and his family
- His failure to deal with the issue of anger
- His failure to admit that he was a workaholic
- His unwillingness, even now, to get help
- His unwise perception that life without his family can be rewarding
- His failure to be honest with himself
- His willingness to hide within his star status at Techworks.

Bill compromised himself by believing a favorite lie of the enemy that many Christians buy into every day. This deception tells us that adoration from others and personal accomplishments can satisfy our soul. This is the reason marriages are falling apart in our churches, and integrity, coupled with holy living, have become more difficult to find. It's much easier to live in a fantasy world where we're the king because it's more difficult to deal with the reality of everyday life. When we trade a God-created reality that may be full of pain but is meant for our growth for a world-based lifestyle that only puffs us up, we have failed to "trade up" and true joy won't last.

Samuel retreated to his study after preaching during two services, exhausted. He had laid himself on the line when he spoke, so he didn't have much to offer after he was through. *At least I made it through the handshakes,* he thought. *If there had been one more...*

There was a knock on his office door. He eased himself up from his chair and looked through his window. The timing couldn't have been worse. He was tired, and this was his worst critic. Samuel took a deep breath and opened the door. The man entered and immediately sat down in the chair to the right of his pastor's desk. Without as much as a hello, he started a verbal attack on Samuel.

He began with a criticism of Samuel's prayer: "How could you leave out the President? Don't you know that we're in a war?" Then, he criticized his introduction: "You shouldn't put pictures of celebrities on the screen. This is church." Finally, he disagreed with the theological premise of his sermon: "How can you say that a Christian can go on sinning? If someone sins all of the time, they must not be a Christian at all."

Samuel waited for the deluge to end and then graciously excused the man. He locked his office door and headed for the restaurant, where he would meet his family for lunch. *I hate ministry,* he thought to himself. *All I do is try to help people, be a little creative, ask the Holy Spirit to lead me, and all I get is grief.* He started to get angry as he drove his car into the restaurant parking lot.

He tried to smile for his wife and tapped his three children on the head. Samuel hated to bring his work home with him, but lately that was getting harder to do. It seemed that he was so full of angry emotions that there was no room for real joy to squeeze through. His wife could tell he was struggling, but she waited until they got home to talk to him about his feelings.

"What's wrong, honey?" Laney asked as she rubbed his shoulders.

"George," Samuel replied.

"What about him?" Linda knew what was coming. She also knew that Samuel needed to vent.

"It's always the same old thing. I can't do anything right," Samuel said. Laney could feel his shoulders tighten.

"That's not how others feel," she reassured him.

"How do you know?" Samuel was skeptical.

His wife continued, "Because the people tell me that they love you."

"Why don't they tell me?" he asked.

"I don't know, but trust me, they like you a lot." Laney kissed him on the cheek and went to look after the kids.

Samuel didn't believe what Laney had just told him. He rarely received an encouraging letter or an "atta boy" from an elder. Ministry was becoming nothing but work; the joy had disappeared a long time ago. He couldn't continue to live like this. He would either change churches, get out of the ministry completely, or fix whatever was wrong with him. Samuel was wise enough to do the latter option. He picked up the phone to call an old friend.

Pastor Horace Houston was a wonderful mentor to Samuel. The two men met while Samuel interned at Pastor Houston's church during his seminary days. Horace noticed Samuel's potential immediately and spent many hours with him. His work had paid off, so he was always glad when Samuel called.

"Hello," Horace answered with that familiar raspy voice. "This is Pastor Houston. Can I help you?"

"I'm not sure, but you always try," replied Samuel.

"Samuel! It's so good to hear from you. How are you, my son?"

"I guess I'm all right." Samuel's hesitancy was not lost on Horace.

"What's wrong, Samuel?" he asked with a concerned tone.

"Nothing that can't be fixed, I guess. I'm just…"

"Just what?" Horace pressed him.

"I'm just a little frustrated. No, I'm a *lot* frustrated. Horace, I don't think I can do this anymore. I'm not kidding. I've decided to leave the ministry." There was a pause.

"Now, hold on, Samuel. What brought this on?" Horace asked.

Samuel decided to vent. "There's no joy in my ministry. I hate going to work. I try my best, but everyone just beats up on me. I'm depressed because Laney and the kids are getting the brunt of it. It's just not working." He waited for Horace to speak. He wasn't sure what his mentor would say, but his response surprised him.

"How many hours a week do you spend with Him?" his mentor asked.

"Who are you referring to?" Samuel asked, confused.

"Christ. How much time do you spend with the Lord?" Horace sounded firm and a bit impatient.

Samuel could hear a phone ringing in the background. "Do you need to get that?"

"No, I'm fine. How much time?"

"Not enough," Samuel was ashamed to say.

"Ten minutes each day? Twenty minutes? An hour? How much time do you spend with Him?" Pastor Houston's persistence made Samuel squirm.

"Not even that much. I spend maybe an hour a week with God. You know, there's the kids, and those phone calls…" Horace didn't let Samuel finish.

"Stop right there." The older man's voice softened. "Samuel, you're in a spiritual war. Satan is trying to rip you apart by stealing your joy. How can you possibly fight when you have no ammunition?"

Samuel knew he was right. "What should I do about it?"

"Start now. Promise me that when you hang up the phone, you will spend fifteen minutes in prayer. Start by praising God for being God. Then, ask Him to bless you. You are the center of Satan's attention. Pray for the spiritual protection, unity, and joy of your family. Pray for your church. Pray again for the same three things. Then offer all of yourself to Him. Finally, offer other things that are on your heart. Okay?"

"Okay."

"Do that every day and then call me in two weeks. Tell me if you feel the same way. If you do, I will help you get out of the ministry. Fair enough?"

"Fair enough," replied Samuel.

"I love you, my son."

"I love you too, Horace. Thank you for taking my call." Samuel hung up the phone and began to pray.

Horace sat back and knew that if Samuel prayed, the phone call in two weeks would bring good news.

Samuel's quest for temporal satisfaction took on these forms:

- His attempt to receive joy from how his congregation felt about him
- His failure to spend adequate time with the Lord
- His failure to pray for his own needs
- His false belief that no one cared about him
- His failure to listen to and trust his wife.

Like Samuel, many of us lose out on joy because we forget about our own spiritual needs. Prayer is often the key ingredient to keep our focus on eternity. It's a good thing to pray for God to bless me. As a pastoral leader, I know that I'm the first domino. If I fall, many others will be affected. In some ways, I'm the first line of defense. Satan wants to steal my joy as a pastor, and discouragement is one of his favorite tools.

An intentional and consistent prayer life can reap huge rewards in this life and for all eternity. Prayer can happen anywhere. I pray when I walk my dog. This daily activity gives me 45 minutes and three miles of stillness. Others pray at their bedsides. Some talk with the Lord at their desk before work. But there is one thing we all have in common: without prayer, we're unarmed. When we're unarmed, we will get killed. Our joy will be stolen, and its lasting effects will slip through our fingers.

What about you? You can begin to "trade up" and find lasting joy when you answer the following questions:

1. How important to you is the adoration of others?
2. Do you fail to confront others because of fear?
3. Are you a different person in public than you are in private?
4. What things do you draw joy from, other than Christ? These things may be fine, but check and see if anything is out of balance.
5. Do you stay at work because you receive kudos there?
6. Do you live for the rush of success?
7. Are you willing to deal with joy-killers like anger, avoidance, and low self-esteem?
8. Does Satan discourage you? In what ways does he do this?
9. Do you pray? How often do you pray?
10. Do you have a consistent way of praying? (Notice the template that Pastor Houston gave to Samuel. This design for prayer works well for me.)

Notes:

_____

_____

_____

_____

_____

_____

_____

_____

_____

_____

_____

_____

_____

_____

_____

A Prayer for Joy that Lasts:

Father, there are many things on earth that bring joy. The enemy wants me to dive in and choose the things that give me immediate satisfaction. However, these things will most likely leave me empty. Teach me to run to You. Teach me to pray, to be real, vulnerable, honest, and submissive. Show me how to keep my eyes on eternity. Lord, satisfy my soul. Please give me lasting joy. Amen.

> *With all prayer and petition pray at all times in the Spirit,*
> *and with this in view, be on the alert with all*
> *perseverance and petition for all the saints.*
> *With all prayer and petition pray at all times in the Spirit,*
> *and with this in view, be on the alert with all perseverance*
> *and petition for all the saints.*

Ephesians 6:18

24. *The Reader's Digest Great Encyclopedic Standard College Dictionary,* (Pleasantville, New York: Readers Digest Association, 1966, 1968, 1971), sv. "Joy".

25. John Piper, *How Is God's Love Experienced in the Heart?*, November 30, 1999, ©Desiring God, www.desiringGod.org, mail@desiringGod.org., toll free: 888.346.4700.

26. John Piper, *How is God's Love Experienced in the Heart?*, November 30, 1999.

27. Lambert Dolphin, *Stumbling Blocks and Milestones,* June 13, 2006, *www.ldolphin.org*

8 When I *Trade Up* I Can Reign with Christ!

I met Jackie Joyner-Kersee while covering the 1990 U.S. Olympic Festival in Minneapolis for a local radio station. This event serves as a try-out for an upcoming Olympic games. In this case, the prize was a trip to Barcelona in 1992.

In her prime, Jackie was often regarded as the best all-around female athlete in the world, along with being the all-time greatest heptathlete since 1986. She won five Olympic medals, and she still holds the American record for the long jump.

Undoubtedly the biggest star in town, Jackie was rarely alone. This morning, I happened to find her by herself, stretching in the middle of the track's infield. I approached her and struck up a conversation. We talked about the incredible skill that's involved with throwing the javelin. I pinched myself to make sure I wasn't dreaming about learning Olympic hints from the greatest female athlete in the world.

Over the years, I've met and interviewed many athletes like Jackie Joyner-Kersee. From track star Michael Johnson to former Green Bay Packer great Bronko Nagurski, these superstars had one thing in common: they wanted to win. They gave their entire careers to winning championships. Many athletes have won several titles. When they taste the fruit of victory, they realize that their work was worthwhile.

The work can be difficult. I remember watching the New York Giants football team grind through their Friday work-out before a

Sunday game at their stadium. They didn't want to be there because it was windy and cold. Yet, they had their eye on the prize. On Sunday they would face the Arizona Cardinals. Their preparation would be necessary to bring them a victory, so the promise of this reward kept them going.

The same can be said about our daily walk with God. There are times when the Christian life is sheer drudgery; however, we can maximize our lives by living for eternal treasure. Let's examine seven key points that, when understood, will help us stand before the *bema* with confidence and gain extravagant rewards there.

1. *The reward system outlined in the Bible is not dependent on works-based salvation.*
The Bible teaches that when we accept Jesus Christ as our personal Savior, we are saved for all time. We can't lose our salvation because we didn't earn it; it's a free gift from God. Chitwood gives us this wonderful explanation of God's grace: "Eternal life is the free 'gift of God,' obtained completely apart from works. Nothing which man does — not one single act, either before or after he becomes a recipient of this life—can have anything at all to do with his salvation, for he has been saved solely by grace through faith; and his salvation is based entirely on the work of Another. Christ's finished work at Calvary provides a means of salvation which fallen man can avail himself of through one revealed means alone: through receiving that which has already been accomplished on his behalf. Works are involved in man's presently possessed eternal salvation, but not man's works. Rather, they are the works of the One Who procured this salvation. Ruined man himself is totally incapable of works. He can't operate in the spiritual realm, for he is 'dead [spiritually] in trespasses and sins' (Eph. 2:1). Thus, since redeemed man had nothing to do with bringing to pass his presently possessed eternal salvation, he can never be brought into any type of judgment where the issue surrounds that which he acquired through Christ's finished work at Calvary. A judgment of this nature would not only be judging that which man had nothing to do with, but it would also be judging once again that which

God has already judged. God judged sin at Calvary in the person of His Son, and God is satisfied."[28]

In the Old Testament, believers offered either animal or flour sacrifices to priests as payment for the penalty incurred by sin. This would assure them that they maintained a right relationship with God, but it didn't secure their salvation. Even during that time, the grace of God was always the guarantor of salvation. Abraham was declared righteous, not because he did all of the right things, but because He believed in God's promises: "Then he believed in the LORD; and He reckoned it to him as righteousness" (Genesis 15:6). Paul said: "For by grace you have been saved through faith; and that not of yourselves, it is the gift of God;…" (Ephesians 2:8). We're saved through faith in Jesus Christ. Upon our acceptance of His gift of mercy, our faith can never be taken from us: "For I am convinced that neither death, nor life, nor angels, nor principalities, nor things present, nor things to come, nor powers, nor height, nor depth, nor any other created thing, will be able to separate us from the love of God, which is in Christ Jesus our Lord" (Romans 8:38, 39).

Other verses that speak about the security of salvation include 2 Corinthians 5:17-19; Ephesians 1:6, Titus 3:5-7; 1 Peter 1:5; and Revelation 21:27, along with this wonderful reminder of the Holy Spirit's seal of salvation: "For as many as are the promises of God, in Him they are yes; therefore also through Him is our Amen to the glory of God through us. Now He who establishes us with you in Christ and anointed us is God, who also sealed us and gave us the Spirit in our hearts as a pledge" (2 Corinthians 1:20-22). We are saved by our belief in Jesus (John 3:16), and our salvation can never be taken away. Even our poor choices can't loosen the Holy Spirit's grip on our heart.

Zane Hodges expands on the wonderful truth of eternal security: "A careful consideration of the offer of salvation, as Jesus Himself presented it, will show that assurance is inherent in that offer. One forceful example of this is John 5:24: "Most assuredly, I say to you, he who hears My word and believes in Him who sent Me has everlasting life, and shall not come into judgment, but has passed from death into life." Anyone who takes this statement at face value should be able to say, 'I know I have everlasting life.

I know I will not come into judgment.'"[29] We are saved by our belief in Jesus. When we accept that Jesus came from Heaven, died on the Cross for our sin, and paid the penalty for our sin, then the Holy Spirit indwells us forever. Nothing can ever change that fact.

After receiving our salvation experience, which is known as "justification" or becoming right with God, our goal is to obey Jesus and become more like Him: this is when obedience, hard work, and spiritual discipline become benchmarks for us. It's during this process called "sanctification" that eternal rewards can be won or lost.

2. *Only believers in Jesus Christ will receive eternal rewards.*
This is a vitally important point. There will be separate judgments for believers and non-believers. The judgment for non-believers is called "The Great White Throne Judgment" which takes place at the very end of recorded time. This is not the *bema,* the judgment for believers. After this judgment, Satan and all of those who are being judged will be thrown into Hell forever. The apostle John records a prophecy of this event in the book of Revelation: "Then I saw a great white throne and Him who sat upon it, from whose presence earth and heaven fled away, and no place was found for them. And I saw the dead, the great and the small, standing before the throne, and books were opened; and another book was opened, which is the book of life; and the dead were judged from the things which were written in the books, according to their deeds. And the sea gave up the dead which were in it, and death and Hades gave up the dead which were in them; and they were judged, every one of them according to their deeds. Then death and Hades were thrown into the lake of fire. This is the second death, the lake of fire. And if anyone's name was not found written in the book of life, he was thrown into the lake of fire" (Revelation 20:11-15). Sadly, those who fail to accept the invitation of Jesus Christ will be eternally damned to hell. This will take place at the Great White Throne Judgment, where'll be no second chance.

Thankfully for us, there'll be another judgment, called the *bema,* for believers. This is the event that we've been looking forward to in this book. We won't be giving an account regarding our salvation, but rather one about our obedience.

Most scholars, including J. Dwight Pentecost, believe that the *bema* will take place immediately following the "Rapture of the Church." The Rapture is the next major biblical event that will happen in the future. Jesus will call His people from earth and move them to a heavenly place; then the judgment for believers will follow immediately. Pentecost writes, "The event herein described takes place immediately following the translation of the church out of this earth's sphere. There are several considerations that support this. In the first place, according to Luke 14:14, reward is associated with resurrection...reward must be a part of the program...When the Lord returns to earth with His bride to reign, the bride is seen to be already rewarded (Rev. 19:8)."[30] We'll stand before Jesus.

It will happen quickly. No one knows when the Rapture will happen (Mark 13:33), but this glorious event will take place: "For the Lord Himself will descend from heaven with a shout, with the voice of the archangel and with the trumpet of God; and the dead in Christ will rise first. Then we who are alive and remain will be caught up together with them in the clouds to meet the Lord in the air, and so we shall always be with the Lord. Therefore comfort one another with these words" (1 Thessalonians 4:16-18). Paul used these words to comfort Christians. We shouldn't be afraid because the Rapture will lead to the *bema,* which will be a wonderful time. We'll see Christ! Our knowledge of this brings us to another vital point.

3. *Rewards will be distributed fairly.*
The Lord will be fair. The prophet Isaiah makes this point in poetic fashion: "The Spirit of the Lord will rest on Him, the spirit of wisdom and understanding, the spirit of counsel and strength, the spirit of knowledge and the fear of the Lord. And He will delight in the fear of the Lord, and He will not judge by what His eyes see, nor make a decision by what His ears hear; but with righteousness He will judge the poor, and decide with fairness for the afflicted of the earth;..." (Isaiah 11:2-4). Jesus said this about Himself: "I can do nothing on My own initiative. As I hear, I

judge; and My judgment is just, because I do not seek My own will, but the will of Him who sent Me" (John 5:30).

Paul Helm emphasizes the justice that will take place at the bema: "For what the Christian doctrine of judgment presupposes is that a person's eternal relation to God will be determined wholly by his past at the time of judgment. God will reach back into a person's life to retrieve buried memories and half-forgotten desires, and he will bring these to an accurate and utterly faithful assessment at the bar of divine justice...Divine justice is thus dispensed in accordance with what a person was and is, and not with what he may become or will become.[31] This idea of absolute justice may strike fear into us; however, the fairness of Christ will exonerate as well as vindicate us.

There'll be no more secrets, so it will be a refreshing time. Everything will be brought out into the open, so we won't have to pretend anymore. Everyone will see our good deeds. Even though they were done in secret, God-pleasing acts will be applauded. An overly negative view of self will be erased forever. Pride will be humbled, and truth will win the day.

Many Christians struggle because they don't feel appreciated. Their work at church goes unnoticed. Their care for an elderly parent goes unseen. Hard work to maintain a struggling marriage is scoffed at by our culture, and saying no to a child brings an onslaught of difficulties.

The Lord is watching. He sees everything you do, and one day, He'll vindicate you. Keep doing His work, and don't be afraid. One day the Lord will expose all of your works. We'll all give an account for our wrongs, but we'll also be rewarded for the right things we did. The *bema* offers a future hope of unimaginable proportions.

How do we earn eternal rewards? Let's remember Joe Wall's insights, highlighted in chapter six:

(1) Invest in the lives of those who minister the Word... (Galatians 6:6, 7).
(2) Minister to those in need... (Matthew 10:42).
(3) Sacrifice to follow Christ... (Matthew 19:27-29).
(4) Give without fanfare... (Matthew 6:1).
(5) Accept abuse for the sake of Christ... (Matthew 5:11,12).

(6) Pray in secret... (Matthew 6:6).

(7) Engage in spiritual activity without fanfare... (Matthew 6:16-18).

(8) Love your enemies by being willing to help them... (Luke 6:35).

(9) Give hearty service to the Lord and not just to please men... (Colossians 3:23, 24).

(10) Entertain those who cannot repay you... (Luke 14:12-14).

Obviously, rewards are based on our service. It's self-denial that will earn us rewards at the *bema*. Despite the popular teaching of today, a Christian can't have all that this world offers and expect to stand strong in eternity. Jesus said: "Do not store up for yourselves treasures on earth, where moth and rust destroy, and where thieves break in and steal. But store up for yourselves treasures in heaven, where neither moth nor rust destroys, and where thieves do not break in or steal; for where your treasure is, there your heart will be also" (Matthew 6:19-21). It's one or the other. Where is *your* heart?

The great Jonathan Edwards, considered by many to be the most intelligent theologian who has ever lived, wondered why we spend so much time on worldly passions: "We are willing to seek earthly things, of trifling value, with great diligence, and through much difficulty; it therefore certainly becomes us to seek that with great earnestness which is of infinitely greater worth and excellence."[32] For most of us, this life takes too much of our time, so we need a priority adjustment. Rewards will be waiting at the *bema* for those who can live without the false cisterns offered by the world.

Once again, salvation is not negotiated at the *bema*. We receive eternal life as a free gift from God by accepting the fact that only Jesus Christ is our Savior. Our salvation is eternal, while rewards are based on our service on earth. All of the items listed above take on a sobering reality when we realize who will be handing out our rewards.

4. *God forgives our sin. Our actions are evaluated.*
The Bible is clear that God forgives sin when we repent: "As far as the east is from the west, so far has He removed our transgressions from us"

(Psalm 103:12). If God has *removed our transgressions from us,* for what are we being judged at the *bema?*

Evaluation at the *bema* isn't punitive, or disciplinary. Christ paid the penalty for any sin that we commit before and after we become a Christian. We'll forfeit rewards which we could have received, but we won't be punished in the judicial sense of "paying" for our sins.

The *bema* has three major purposes. (1) This judgment will evaluate the quality of our work (1 Corinthians 3:13-15). Everything we do is either acceptable and thus worthy of rewards, or unacceptable. (2) The *bema* will destroy and remove unacceptable things that we have produced in our lives. The apostle Paul portrayed these as wood, hay, and stubble, which are easily destroyed by fire. (3) On the other hand, Jesus will also reward our kingdom-building work and attitudes, represented by gold, silver, and precious stones. These will be tested by fire and won't be consumed.

Not only did Paul lay the foundation for the *bema* in 1 Corinthians 3, but he also wrote, "Therefore do not go on passing judgment before the time, but wait until the Lord comes who will both bring to light the things hidden in the darkness and disclose the motives of men's hearts; and then each man's praise will come to him from God" (1 Corinthians 4:5). The Bible clearly teaches that the nature of our hearts will be evaluated.

Will we experience shame or regret at the *bema?* Yes. Some Christians will receive more rewards than others because all of our actions have eternal consequences. Paul made this clear to Timothy: "If we endure, we will also reign with Him; if we deny Him, He also will deny us; if we are faithless, He remains faithful, for He cannot deny Himself" (2 Timothy 2:12, 13). Our choices made during this life will clearly make a difference at the *bema.*

Sadly, some may be considered unworthy to rule. Jesus made this point clearly in this parable:

"For it is just like a man about to go on a journey, who called his own slaves and entrusted his possessions to them. To one he gave five talents, to another, two, and to another, one, each according to his own ability; and he went on his journey. Immediately the one who had received the five talents went and traded with them, and gained five more talents. In the same manner the one who had received the two talents gained two more. But he who received the one talent went away, and dug a hole in the ground and hid his master's money. Now after a long time the master of those slaves came and settled accounts with them. The one who had received the five talents came up and brought five more talents, saying, 'Master, you entrusted five talents to me. See, I have gained five more talents.' His master said to him, 'Well done, good and faithful slave. You were faithful with a few things, I will put you in charge of many things; enter into the joy of your master.' Also the one who had received the two talents came up and said, 'Master, you entrusted two talents to me. See, I have gained two more talents.' His master said to him, 'Well done, good and faithful slave. You were faithful with a few things, I will put you in charge of many things; enter into the joy of your master.' And the one also who had received the one talent came up and said, 'Master, I knew you to be a hard man, reaping where you did not sow and gathering where you scattered no seed. And I was afraid, and went away and hid your talent in the ground. See, you have what is yours.' But his master answered and said to him, 'You wicked, lazy slave, you knew that I reap where I did not sow and gather where I scattered no seed. Then you ought to have put my money in the bank, and on my arrival I would have received my money back with interest. Therefore take away the talent from him, and give it to the one who has the ten talents.' For to everyone who has, more shall be given, and he will have an abundance; but from the one who does not have, even what he does have shall be taken away. Throw out the worthless slave into the outer darkness; in that place there will be weeping and gnashing of teeth'" (Matthew 25:14-30).

Two servants were rewarded for being faithful. Each was given authority over more things as their compensation; however, the cowardly slave didn't receive an inheritance. Other New Testament passages point to this same truth. Paul speaks about being "disqualified" for not running the race by the rules in 1 Corinthians 9:27. Some will be disqualified for kingship at the *bema*. They'll still be in heaven, but they'll have been *saved as through fire.*

This truth doesn't contradict verses such as Revelation 7:17: "…God shall wipe every tear from their eyes" or Revelation 21:4: "…there shall no longer be any mourning, or crying, or pain." This perfect peace will be evident in our eternal state. The *bema* will take place before the Lord's one-thousand-year reign on earth. Sin will rear its ugly head at the end of this glorious time (Revelation 20:7). Some people will turn against God before Satan is defeated. At that time, the Great White Throne Judgment will usher in an eternal state of joy and gladness for us.

We'll experience a moment of regret at the *bema* for the times we chose to drink from broken wells; however, this regret will be short-lived. Our time at the *bema* will be filled with joy because of God's grace. We will look forward to a magnificent life in heaven.

E. Schuyler English writes, "Joy will indeed be the predominant emotion of life with the Lord; but I suspect that, when our works are made manifest at the tribunal, some grief will be mixed with the joy, and we shall know shame as we suffer loss. But we shall rejoice also as we realize that the rewards given will be another example of the grace of our Lord; for at best we are unprofitable servants."[33]

Think of the *bema* like you would a time of accomplishment in your life. It might be your graduation from high school or college. At the ceremony, you probably felt some measure of disappointment and remorse that you didn't work harder. You may have felt pain because you didn't take full advantage of opportunities. At the same time, joy was most likely the predominant emotion that you were feeling. You didn't leave weeping because of your grades; you were just grateful and full of joy because you graduated!

This is a fine line to walk when we consider the *bema*. To overdo the aspect of sorrow undermines the grace of God, but to underestimate its effect destroys any reason to remain faithful. The important thing to remember is that we'll give an account to Jesus for our deeds. We can change our lives when we make decisions based on this knowledge.

5. *Rewards will most likely come in the form of authority.*

Rewards will be literal; they're not a mystical concept. Dillow says, "One day, the Scriptures everywhere affirm, the struggle of fallen man will finally come to an end. This consummation will not be achieved by social engineering or by the successful implantation of any human ideology. Rather it will be accomplished by a supernatural intervention of God in history, the second coming of Christ. Finally, history will receive a worthy outcome—the Kingdom of God. Page after page of Scripture speaks of this glorious future and the possibility that those who are Christ's servants now can achieve positions of honor in that future glory then. These positions of honor are an important aspect of the believer's inheritance."[34] The system of rewards began at the beginning of creation. God created man to reign over creation (Genesis 1:28-30). Unfortunately, because of sin, man lost his position. However, David tells us that God still intends us to have authority in Christ's future kingdom: "When I consider Your heavens, the work of Your fingers, the moon and the stars, which You have ordained; what is man that You take thought of him and the son of man that You care for him? Yet You have made him a little lower than God, and You crown him with glory and majesty! You make him to rule over the works of Your hands; You have put all things under his feet, all sheep and oxen, and also the beasts of the field, the birds of the heavens and the fish of the sea, whatever passes through the paths of the seas" (Psalm 8:3-8). The author of Hebrews reiterates these thoughts in chapter 2, verses 5-8.

God clearly intends man to have kingly authority in the future. There are many other verses that speak of our royal future, including Genesis 17:6; 35:11; Exodus 19:6; and Revelation 1:6; 5:10; 20:4.

The Bible teaches that we will reign under the leadership of Christ. He will be the head of this governmental structure: "…and He is the Head over all rule and authority" (Colossians 2:10). This makes logical sense. Christ is the head of the Church (Ephesians 5:23). Colossians 1:17 tells us that He holds all creation together. He will also be the leader of His people in the eternal state.

The most exciting part of our future kingship is the knowledge that we'll be with Jesus. The Lord made this very clear: "Then Peter said to

Him, "Behold, we have left everything and followed You; what then will
there be for us?" And Jesus said to them, "Truly I say to you, that you
who have followed Me, in the regeneration when the Son of Man will sit
on His glorious throne, you also shall sit upon twelve thrones, judging
the twelve tribes of Israel" (Matthew 19:27-28). Jesus desires that His disciples reign with Him.

This is a difficult concept for us to understand. We've been taught to
earn the love of Jesus, but there's something inside of us that tells us we
fall short. It's life-changing, however, to consider the fact that Jesus wants
us to rule with Him. When we accept the Lord's love for us, then we're
free to be ourselves: we can be who He created us to be. We may not fit
into a mold or be like everyone else, but that doesn't matter. The Lord
loves us and wants to reign with us. This awesome thought is expanded
upon by Kenneth Quick: "Jesus desires that the disciples enter into a
kingly fellowship with Him. They will sit with Him (Luke 22:28-30)
and dine with Him, sharing not just the administration of His kingdom
but the intimate presence of the King. Those that attain this level of significance work with Him, and beside Him, as He rules. They share the
intimate fellowship of those who have a common vocation. They are true
co-regents."[35]

Many times when we travel in a large group, we line up and create a
caravan. The leader moves out into the front, and then we follow along
because we trust that he knows where to go.

In a very real sense, we're following our leader, Jesus Christ, directly
to a throne of leadership. Sadly, many of us will not be willing to follow
in His footsteps because Jesus endured suffering and death. Even when
our lives get hard, however, we can still follow Him. If we're not afraid of
the pain, the result of suffering will maximize our lives. Peter wrote, "For
you have been called for this purpose, since Christ also suffered for you,
leaving you an example for you to follow in His steps…And after you
have suffered for a little while, the God of grace, who called you to His
eternal glory in Christ, will Himself perfect, confirm, strengthen, and
establish you" (1 Peter 2:21; 5:10). We are being trained by suffering on
earth to rule in eternity. Jesus told the apostle John: "He who overcomes,

I will grant to him to sit down with Me on My throne, as I also overcame and sat down with My Father on His throne" (Revelation 3:21).

The Arizona Cardinals football team holds its annual training camp in Flagstaff, Arizona. Of course, this allows the team to get out of the sizzling Arizona desert, but there's another good reason to train in that locale. The thin air in Flagstaff makes it the perfect place to get in shape. When a team trains at nine thousand feet, a game played at normal sea level seems easy. Physical conditioning is more productive in the mountains. None of the National Football League training camps are easy for the players. Whether if they're in Flagstaff or any other city in the nation, these players work until they've got nothing left to offer. They understand that pre-season training will make them more physically fit for game day.

For us, suffering has an eternal purpose: it prepares us believers to reign on an eternal throne. God is watching how we handle our trials. Those of us who give up will be given less, but those of us who endure will gain virtue and perspective. More importantly, those who persevere will gain an eternal throne. Robert H. Mounce describes the believer's ascent to the throne: "The martyrs in Revelation 6:10 cried out for vindication. It is to be fully realized when the overcomers take their place beside the Lamb on His throne. Their victory and consequent exaltation follow the pattern of the victory of Christ, who also overcame and sat down with his Father on the heavenly throne."[36]

An understanding of our eternal destiny has obvious ramifications in the lives of us as believers. Why would anyone trade an eternal throne for a blond bimbo? Why would we give up a dinner with Jesus to watch porn on the Internet? What right-minded person would throw away an opportunity to rule in eternity for a few extra bucks and a promotion at an earthly job?

When eternity is kept in mind, sin becomes an *either-or* proposition. Every time we choose to disobey God, we give up something in eternity. We can either "trade up," or miss out. Our behavior and motives decide our place in heaven, which should be a sobering thought for any Christian. Our appointment to eternal positions takes place at the *bema,* where all of us Christians will appear. What right-minded person would throw away an opportunity to rule in eternity while engaged in a destructive and self-centered drive to earn a few extra bucks and a promotion at an earthly job?

Where will we reign? We will certainly reign over the earth during the one-thousand year reign of Christ. Remember, judgment at the *bema* will take place immediately following the Rapture of the Church and just before Jesus comes back to reign on earth for 1,000 years. This is called His "Millennial Reign." During this time period, those found worthy will reign with Jesus from the Temple Mount in the city of Jerusalem. The apostle John wrote: Blessed and holy is the one who has a part in the first resurrection; over these the second death has no power, but they will be priests of God and of Christ and will reign with Him for a thousand years" (Revelation 20:6). *We* are the priests.

Quick elaborates, "The earth is the clearest object to come under the rule of the crowned saints. Genesis 1:28-30 and Psalm 8 declare that God intends for men to rule over the earth and all it contains. Jesus will return and bring the Kingdom to earth. The earth will probably be divided geographically, proportionate to the faithfulness of these servants. One can visualize kings and queens over continents, over groupings of nations, over single nations, over tribes, over districts, over cities, and over towns. Each king will have proven himself worthy of whatever position he serves. Along with the position will also go a degree of access into the presence of the King of Kings."[37] Quick also believes that this reign may extend much further. We could even be reigning over the entire universe.

The Bible is also clear that we'll rule over angels (1 Corinthians 6:3), which is an amazing truth. The grace of God can be clearly seen; He loves and respects us so much that we'll rule over heavenly beings who are presently more powerful than men.

It's important to respect yourself. Don't let Satan convince you that you're worthless by letting him destroy your future or your body. You can *rule* with Christ. Keep that thought in mind. Tape it on your mirror or stick it on your fridge. Tell yourself every day, *I can rule with Christ*, then temptations will become less attractive.

6. *Crowns will be given to faithful believers.*

The Scriptures clearly teach that crowns will also be issued to faithful believers. Many see the quest for rewards as a selfish pursuit. In order to justify this belief, some Christians have unknowingly misinterpreted an important passage of Scripture. Revelation 4:10-12 states, "The twenty-four elders will fall down before Him who sits on the throne, and will worship Him who lives forever and ever, and will cast their crowns before the throne, saying, 'Worthy are You, our Lord and our God, to receive glory and honor and power; for You created all things, and because of Your will they existed, and were created.'"

Will we throw our crowns back at the feet of Jesus? Will we all be equal after doing this humble gesture? Quick rightly defines four reasons why this won't be the case: "First...the passage has nothing to do with the judgment seat or the receiving of crowns. The elders already possess the crowns when they appear before the Lord. Second...supposing the elders are identified with the church is a most unlikely possibility. Third, even if they are representatives of the church, the action of the twenty-four elders is intimately linked with the worship of the four living creatures. The four creatures initiate the worship by giving glory to God, and the elders respond by falling down and casting their crowns before His throne. The point is that the action of casting crowns is pictured as occurring over and over, and is not a once and for all action. Their worship always takes this form. Fourth, though they cast their crowns before Him, they do no cast their thrones, nor do they give up their position and proximity to Him...this action in no way changes the glory or honor He has bestowed on them. They keep it permanently."[38]

These are good insights. If the twenty-four elders and four living creatures are not believers, then who are they? Mounce believes that they're heavenly beings: "Their song of praise (Rev. 5:9-10) definitely sets them apart from those who were purchased by the blood of Christ (most certainly the Church!)...it seems best to take the twenty-four elders as an exalted angelic order."[39]

7. *It's good to pursue heavenly rewards.*

Believing that we'll throw our crowns away doesn't do justice to the reward system. It isn't wrong or prideful to desire rewards in heaven. We're told to do that. Jesus encouraged His disciples to seek rewards in heaven (Matthew 5:12; 6:1-6; 10:41, 42; 16:24-27; Mark 10:21; Luke 6:23). Joseph Dillow relates this sad story of his own childhood: "The writer well remembers the time when as a new Christian he had just learned about the doctrine of eternal rewards. In youthful fervor he rushed to visit his pastor, only to have his new enthusiasm crushed. 'Do you mean to tell me,' he replied, 'that there will be distinctions in heaven? God does not show partiality!'[40] That pastor was wrong. Dillow elaborates, "It is sometimes asked, 'How can future chastisement have any motivational influence on our lives now?' We answer that throughout Scripture God has used warnings about the future to promote the sanctification of His people in time. He deemed warnings of these judgments necessary for motivating the indolent and carnal. As their meaningless lives progress, the force of these warnings has more and more impact on them. Having warned them, He must, of course, carry out His chastisement…for many the sobering reality of final accountability in this matter serves as a goad to perseverance and a barrier to backsliding."[41]

Paul used the concept of future rewards as a way to motivate Christians (1 Corinthians 3:8; 9:25). Through a discussion of future rewards, the apostle John warns believers not to stray from the teachings of Jesus: "Watch yourselves, that you do not lose what we have accomplished, but that you may receive a full reward" (2 John 8). Heavenly rewards are to be sought after; they're set before us as a goal. It can be sinful to pursue earthly things, but it's definitely godly to desire heavenly crowns.

Jesus wants to show His incredible love for us by giving us eternal rewards. Because He designed the reward system, it's His desire to carry it out in order to honor us. He'll enjoy giving us our rewards too.

I have a close friend who has done well in the business world. He's the most generous man I know. Over time, I've learned to accept his generosity. He gets great joy from watching me enjoy his gifts. In the same way, the Lord will take great joy in watching His children revel in His generosity for all of eternity.

Jesus accepted the rewards that He was promised. He now sits at the right hand of the Father: "So then, when the Lord Jesus had spoken to them, He was received up into heaven and sat down at the right hand of God." (Mark 16:19). After His ascension back into heaven, Jesus took His proper place of honor. This is what the Father had intended to happen (Isaiah 53:11, 12). Now, He could enjoy His Son forever.

It would be ludicrous to think that Jesus didn't motivate Himself with this truth. He knew that there was a purpose for His suffering. Besides, He would rejoin His Father after completing His mission. He wouldn't deny Himself what was already rightfully His, so He was right in allowing the Father to enjoy His gift to Him. Jesus should be our example.

8. *Seeking rewards and loving Jesus go together.* When was the last time you heard a clear sermon about eternal rewards? They're hard to come by because it seems that very few speakers and authors are willing to tackle the topic. This is largely due to the fact that many people see eternal rewards as a selfish pursuit. They believe that the motive for good deeds is to glorify God, which is true. As we become more like Christ, good deeds come naturally. But many of these same people believe that to do something good in order to seek a reward seems selfish.

This line of thinking couldn't be further from the truth. To seek after the things that Christ provides is the best way to love Him. When we seek after eternal rewards, we begin to see things through the lens of eternity, which will lead us to make decisions that will enhance our lives. These good and righteous choices will help us see the world the way Christ sees it. When we learn to look at the world through His eyes, our deeds will glorify and please Him.

Paul understood this process: "I have been crucified with Christ; and it is no longer I who live, but Christ lives in me; and the life which I now live in the flesh I live by faith in the Son of God, who loved me and gave Himself up for me" (Galatians 2:20). Paul was set on becoming more like Jesus. He was also running for a prize. For Paul, the two pursuits were one in the same.

The Lord instituted the reward system in order to keep our priorities in order. Knowing what awaits us at the *bema* gives us both confidence and hope. Rewards give us a new perspective on God's good and pure love: He desires to reign with His children. Understanding eternal rewards also helps to keep us from making destructive decisions. Rewards are designed to motivate us to obey. Obedience to the Lord's commands means that we love Him: "If you love Me, you will keep My commandments" (John 14:15). Obedience is the only road to eternal rewards. When we obey, we show how much we love Jesus.

Seeking eternal rewards and living our lives to glorify God are one and the same. Good deeds please Christ because becoming more like Him glorifies the Father. Meanwhile, eternal rewards for us are piling up, and they will be distributed at the *bema.*

The biblical evidence for eternal rewards is overwhelming. Earning rewards does not equate to work-based salvation because this process happens only after we have been justified by Christ. Only faithful believers are eligible for rewards, which will come in the form of authority and crowns. Loving Christ means pursuing His eternal gifts that will change our lives now. When we focus on what's ahead, we will "trade up."

In summary, let me give you five important reasons why accepting and understanding eternal rewards maximizes my life:

1. *I can make right choices.*
I am less likely to choose something the world offers me when I understand that in doing so, I will throw away eternal rewards. Let's return to the "blond-bimbo" scenario. Many Christian men decide to leave their wives because they are seeking gratification and adoration from another woman. I wonder if they'd make this choice if they could see their eternal rewards being put back in storage. As wonderful as women are, none of them can compare to reigning and fellowshipping with Christ.

There are others who make similar decisions because they either don't believe in, or have forgotten about, eternal rewards. Some Christians allow bitterness to overwhelm them, which causes them to become worthless to the kingdom. Others gossip in order to feel significant, but they don't understand that real worth and significance awaits them at the *bema.* Some believers don't serve in their local churches because they're too busy; their worldly priorities are causing eternal treasure to fade away.

The author of Hebrews underlines the plight of a believer who is not focused on eternity: "For in the case of those who have once been enlightened and have tasted of the heavenly gift and have been made partakers of the Holy Spirit, and have tasted the good word of God and the powers of the age to come, and then have fallen away, it is impossible to renew them again to repentance, since they again crucify to themselves the Son of God and put Him to open shame. For ground that drinks the rain which often falls on it and brings forth vegetation useful to those for whose sake it is also tilled, receives a blessing from God; but if it yields thorns and thistles, it is worthless and close to being cursed, and it ends up being burned" (Hebrews 6:4-8).

Many believe this passage applies to non-believers; however, the context and the audience support the view that the author is warning believers to keep their minds on Christ. Walvoord and Zuck agree about this: "The author's words suggested a deep hardening of their hearts against all efforts to win them back, not to Christian conversion, but to Christian commitment."[42] It's a dangerous thing to allow our hearts to harden. If we allow ourselves to become unusable for the kingdom, we'll lose vast rewards in the next life.

When I understand and acknowledge the truth of eternal rewards, every portion of my life is affected because every decision is made in light of eternity. When the Holy Spirit nudges me to hug my wife, my response will be accounted for at the *bema*. Failure to discipline my children will be noticed in eternity. Giving money anonymously, even though the temptation to be applauded was strong, will be rewarded by Christ.

Spending time in prayer will lead to a deeper intimacy with Jesus. This intimacy will lead directly to having a throne in the kingdom. Failure to pray could leave me on the outside looking in—not on the outside of heaven—but on the outside of His inner circle. James makes it clear that those who pursue God gain intimate access to Him: "Draw near to God and He will draw near to you" (James 4:8a). Intimacy with Christ in the New Testament was based upon one's willingness to sacrifice earthly treasure in order to follow Him (Luke 14:25-27, 33; Matthew 19:21, 27-30).

Intimacy in the kingdom will be gained the same way (Mark 10:35-40; Revelation 7:14-17). I may not reign with Him if I hold on to earthly treasure. What earthly pursuit could possibly be worth more than spending all of eternity in an intimate relationship with Jesus?

You can begin to learn how to make right choices when you answer the following questions:

A. Am I currently involved with any activity that is disobedience to God? If so, what steps can I take to change my behavior?
B. Is Jesus an intimate friend or a judge-like figure? If He's not an intimate companion, what can I do to find more time with Him?
C. Is there any decision that I'm going to make in the next year that has strong worldly implications, (i.e. more money, a high degree of respect from men), or will lead to a more comfortable lifestyle? If so, how can I guard my heart? How will my choice be perceived at the *bema*?

Notes:

_____
_____
_____
_____
_____
_____
_____
_____

2. *I am accountable.*

My life changes when I acknowledge that my actions will be accounted for. Accountability is a key factor in living a victorious and worthwhile Christian life.

I know a man who has the potential to be a major force for the kingdom. He's a fine speaker, an excellent writer, and a compassionate minister. He has all of the tools to be a kingdom warrior. Unfortunately, he's not allowed himself to become accountable. The only men he will listen to are spread around the country, but he's not accountable to anyone for his day-to-day actions. Now, this man has found himself under church discipline, and his reputation in the community has suffered. His integrity is in question because he wouldn't allow himself to be truly accountable to other men.

Paul showed wisdom in the way that he planted churches by setting up governmental structures that would keep leaders accountable. Unfortunately, many of today's leaders have not followed the apostle's example. Too many pastors are left unaccountable. Many times this *pastor-king* syndrome results in sexual sin, pride, and discouragement.

A recent editorial article in *Christianity Today* magazine speaks to this problem: "A pervasive culture of sensuality and disregard for communal accountability guarantees that some pastors will struggle with all sorts of sexual temptation. Toss into this mix the Internet's availability and anonymity, which have spread the reach of pornography and clandestine sexual encounters. The challenge to help our pastors resist temptation demands a wise church response."[43] The writer points to Billy Graham's response as a model for others: "Evangelist Billy Graham knew many leaders who succumbed to temptation on the preaching circuit. That's why in 1948, Graham met with his evangelistic team in Modesto, California, and discussed how to protect themselves against smearing the gospel of Christ. They brainstormed the particular temptations faced by traveling evangelists and identified wealth, prestige, slander, and sex. They fought back by setting rigorous standards: They would not meet, travel, or eat alone with any woman but their wives. The rule created some awkward moments. Graham relented a bit and in 1993 ate with then-First Lady Hillary Clinton at a table in the center of a restaurant. But the rules worked. The so-called Modesto Manifesto protected the men against their ignoble impulses and helped rehabilitate the image of gospel preachers."[44]

Billy Graham wisely understood that all believers need accountability. We're all sinners who can't trust ourselves. We need other Christians to keep us accountable at a deeper level. The Bible calls for *community* among us believers because living within a community helps us to see ourselves the way we really are. This is why it's so important to be involved in a church. It's also wise to find a close group of friends with whom we can be vulnerable. Even though it's hard to be vulnerable, we can't open ourselves to accountability if we hide from others.

The truth of the matter is that we will be held accountable anyway when we encounter Jesus at the *bema*. Would we rather have our sins dealt with now, or then? It's a choice that we all make. When we take eternal rewards seriously, it will affect our lives. Our time on earth will be richer, and we'll understand even more the depth of God and how much He loves us. We'll be less likely to practice sin that blocks our fellowship with Him. Eternal accountability is a wonderful truth that will help us if we really embrace it.

You can begin the process of being accountable when you answer the following questions:

A. Do I act differently when I'm alone than I do when I am with others? If so, are these destructive behaviors?
B. Does anyone know everything about me?
C. Do I meet face to face with anyone on a regular basis who is willing to rebuke me for sin?
D. Am I teachable?
E. What steps do I need to take in order to become accountable?
F. Do I take sin seriously?
G. Am I willing to take the necessary steps to become accountable?

Notes:
_____
_____
_____
_____
_____
_____
_____

3. *I am encouraged.*

Life can be discouraging. There are days when I don't think that I've done anything that's worthwhile. On those days, I wonder why God called me to be a pastor because I feel inadequate and don't see any fruit from my ministry. I want to run away and let someone else do it. I'm sure they could do it better.

I'm not alone. Some polls tell us that as many as fifty percent of pastors' marriages end in divorce, fifty percent say they would leave the ministry if they could find another way to make a living, and as many as eighty percent of pastors leave the ministry within five years.[45] These alarming numbers shouldn't surprise us. Discouragement is a difficult thing to overcome: it's everywhere.

Those who possess worldly treasure and fame easily become discouraged, which can lead to suicidal depression. Cleopatra and Mark Antony died by their own hand. Curt Cobain, lead singer of the grunge band Nirvana, was killed by a self-inflicted shotgun wound. Sigmund Freud gave himself a lethal dose of morphine. Other rich and famous people who ended their own lives include Margaux Hemingway, Freddie Prinze, Brian Keith, River Phoenix, and more. Other celebrities find themselves in and out of drug and alcohol rehab facilities. The hurdle of discouragement cannot be avoided by those who have a wealth of earthly goods. Douglas C. Kenney was an American writer who co-founded *National Lampoon* magazine in 1970. His suicide note summed up the human condition: "These are the best days I've chosen to ignore."

Discouragement runs through the Christian community, the secular community, and even through the world of the elite. What is the cause of discouragement? I believe discouragement happens when we take our eyes off of eternal treasure. When we live for today, our lives will disappoint us. Treasures earned in this life will leave us groping for more, but we'll only be fully satisfied by treasures in heaven.

It's during times of discouragement that I become acutely aware of my need to keep my eyes on heaven. Throughout the centuries, believers have been motivated and encouraged by a belief in eternal treasure. Abraham was comforted by God's promise of a future inheritance: "I will give to you and to your descendants after you, the land of your sojournings, all the land of Canaan, for an everlasting possession; and I will be their God"

(Genesis 17:8). David embraced the truth of an eternal reckoning: "The LORD is in His holy temple; the LORD'S throne is in heaven; His eyes behold, His eyelids test the sons of men. The LORD tests the righteous and the wicked, and the one who loves violence His soul hates. Upon the wicked He will rain snares; fire and brimstone and burning wind will be the portion of their cup. For the LORD is righteous, He loves righteousness. The upright will behold His face" (Psalm 11:4-7). Paul sought an eternal prize which included a partnership with Christ: "I do all things for the sake of the gospel, so that I may become a fellow partaker of it. Do you not know that those who run in a race all run, but only one receives the prize? Run in such a way that you may win" (1 Corinthians 9:23, 24).

The hope of eternal treasure is still an encouragement to Christians in modern times. Slaves wrote and sang beautiful songs that spoke of a coming glory. This anthem was used during the Civil War period:

Oh freedom, oh freedom,
Oh freedom over me.
And before I'll be a slave,
I'll be buried in my grave,
And go home to my Lord and be free.

Even the horrors of the Holocaust couldn't stop Dietrich Bonhoeffer from holding on to the truth of coming glory. On Sunday, April 8, 1945, he had just finished conducting a service of worship at Schoenberg when two soldiers came to take him away. As he left, he said to another prisoner, "This is the end—but for me, the beginning of life." He was hanged the next day, less than a week before the Allies reached the camp.

Now, modern martyrs and Christian leaders hang onto the hope of heavenly rewards. An anonymous hymn writer penned these beautiful words:

O Christ, in Thee my soul hath found,
And found in Thee alone,

The peace, the joy I sought so long,
The bliss till now unknown.

I sighed for rest and happiness,
I yearned for them, not Thee;

But while I passed my Saviour by,
His love laid hold on me.

Now none but Christ can satisfy,
None other name for me;

There's love, and life, and lasting joy,
Lord Jesus, found in Thee.

You can be encouraged by your belief in heavenly rewards. Regardless of how bad things get on earth, there is always something to hope for in heaven.

Many pastors have adopted a curriculum called *Men's Fraternity,* written by Robert Lewis, Pastor of Fellowship Bible Church in Little Rock, Arkansas. Within this study, Lewis paints an exciting picture of heaven. Men love it because they are made to work and have adventures. Eternity is a long time. If we picture a heaven without further accomplishments, joy, and excitement, it just isn't appealing.

Many scholars portray heaven as a place of work and reward. The book of Genesis tells us that man was placed in the Garden to work. At the time, man enjoyed his work. As the master over the earth, he was commanded by God to manage it well. Adam then named the animals. When God saw that it wasn't good for him to be alone, He gave him a woman to love. Adam also apparently had a face-to-face relationship with God (Genesis 3:8), unhindered by sin. Life seemed exciting because he was active and working.

Work was easy and enjoyable before man's fall. God cursed man because of his sin, and work became the kind of difficult struggle that we now experience in our lives. God rebuked Adam, saying, "Cursed is the ground because of you; in toil you will eat of it all the days of your life" (Genesis 3:17b).

Think for a moment about a world without sin. The curse will be removed after Christ returns, and we will receive our rewards at the *bema*. We will become eternal beings who will do the things we are created to do. Because we're made to work, we'll work throughout eternity. We're made to accomplish things with our incredible intellectual talents, as well as our athletic and artistic abilities. God is glorified when we use these gifts and even more pleased when we use our bodies to glorify Him (1 Corinthians 6:20). It would be logical to assume that heaven will be a place that we can use our bodies, minds, and souls to their fullest potential. Perhaps heaven will be a return to life as it was in the Garden, when we'll take joy in our work. Each of us will enjoy energizing and robust activities that fit us perfectly.

Wayne Grudem sets forth this incredible view of heaven: "When the author of Hebrews says that we do *not yet* see everything in subjection to man (Hebrews 2:8), he implies that eventually all things will… be subject to us, under the kingship of the man Christ Jesus…. This will fulfill God's original plan to have everything in the world subject to human beings that He had made. In this sense, then, we will *inherit the earth* and reign over it as God originally intended. For that reason it should not strike us as surprising to find that some of the descriptions of life in heaven include features that are very much part of the physical or material creation that God has made. We shall eat and drink at the marriage supper of the Lamb (Revelation 19:9). Jesus will once again drink wine with His disciples in the heavenly kingdom (Luke 22:18). The river of the water of life will flow from the throne of God and of the Lamb through the middle of the street of the city…These things are just some of the excellent features of perfection and final goodness of the physical creation God has made."[46] We can be encouraged that there will be no boredom in heaven.

At the *bema*, our place in heaven will be set. Heaven will be an exciting place where there will be incredible joy. Every moment will be spent doing purposeful things. A faithful Christian will draw more enjoyment out of his eternal experience because he'll be in the position of authority. Not only will we be reigning kings, but we will also be intimate *metochoi* or actual *partners* with Christ.

Be encouraged, and don't give up. A new day is coming when you'll be noticed and acknowledged for the things you've done. Someday, you'll be able to do something that you love to do for all of eternity. You can enhance this experience by getting to know Christ on a more intimate level. When you take your faith seriously, you're setting the table for an incredible eternity. The decisions that you make now will directly affect your eternal state.

Robert Lewis reminds the men in his network to live with eternity in mind. He teaches that we live in a purposeful universe. Life takes on a special purpose when we remember that heaven is real: "Faith decisions are the most important decisions any man will make. Today, I will manage the affairs of my life, one way or the other, believing that somebody sees and is keeping score and somebody sees and wants to help."[47]

You can begin to be encouraged when you answer the following questions:

A. What are the two most discouraging things in my life?
B. Have I consistently prayed about these things?
C. Do I believe that God can help me overcome these obstacles?
D. How often do I think of eternity? Do I have a proper view of eternity?
E. Do I believe that life will completely change in heaven?
F. How close am I to giving up?
G. What would be the consequences if I give up?
H. Can I trust God enough to keep going?
I. Can I commit myself to a deeper life of prayer and Bible study?
J. Am I willing to ask for help?

Notes:

_____

_____

_____

_____

_____

_____

_____

_____

4. *I am motivated to seek a higher Christian life.*

My life is maximized when I strive to go to the next level in my relationship with Jesus. Too many Christians, however, settle for less. There are many church-goers who are simply "putting in their time," but this shouldn't happen if eternal treasure is kept in mind.

Wilma Rudolph learned what it meant to focus on what lies ahead. Born prematurely in 1940, Wilma couldn't be treated at a local hospital because of racial segregation. She was then nursed at home where she fought many illnesses, including measles, mumps, scarlet fever, chicken pox, and double pneumonia. Wilma was finally taken to the doctor when her left leg and foot became weak and deformed. She was diagnosed with polio, and her mother was told that Wilma would never walk again.

But Wilma's mother didn't give up. She eventually found a hospital that would treat her daughter and took Wilma there for treatment twice every week. Even though it was a one-hundred mile round trip, that didn't daunt her. The entire family aided Wilma by learning how to do physical therapy at home. They had their eyes on the prize of Wilma being able to live a normal life. Finally, by the age of twelve, she could walk normally, no longer needing crutches, braces, or corrective shoes.

Wilma Rudolph decided to become an athlete. In high school, she became a basketball star. Her team won a state championship, and Wilma set scoring records. After basketball, she went on to track and field and competed in her first Olympic Games in 1956 at the age of sixteen, winning a bronze medal in the 4x4 relay. The little girl who would never walk again was now an Olympic medalist.

Four years later, her success continued. Wilma became the first American woman to win three gold medals in Olympic competition. Her experience at the Games in Rome made her a celebrated female athlete. She used her success for the good by breaking racial and gender barriers, setting the stage for many black female athletes to come.

Later that year, she was invited by Billy Graham to join Baptist Christian Athletes in Japan. In the same year, she was selected to represent the U.S. State Department as a goodwill ambassador at the Game of Friendship in Dakar.

Her finest moment may have come when she returned to her home-town. Her victory parade in Clarksville, Tennessee, was the first racially integrated event held there. It was the first time in Clarksville history that blacks and whites had gathered together for the same event. She went on to protest segregation laws until all of them were repealed.

The small girl with a crippled leg had dreamed big dreams, realizing there could be more to life if she was willing to work and believe in her-self. Who could have dreamed that not only would she walk again, but that she'd also win four Olympic medals? Wilma Rudolph went for the gold and got it.

We're all motivated by future rewards. A businessman works for the opportunity to build his company into a powerhouse. A student lays it all on the line for a higher grade. A housewife smiles when a friend com-pliments her ability to decorate her home. People everywhere enter contests. From pie-baking contests to bingo games, men and women are consistently looking for something better. It's important for a Christian to look for rewards in the right place.

God gave us legitimate longings to feel significant, loved, cared for, and understood. The only person who can provide that kind of fulfill-ment is Jesus. Intimacy with the King will satisfy our longings. We're motivated when we understand that each decision we make will affect that intimacy. If we think that our ticket of salvation is stamped, and that's all there is to life, we're less likely to break through barriers and go to a higher level.

The Bible encourages us to be motivated by eternal treasure. We've already discussed many of these passages, but one in particular stands out. Paul was passing his torch of leadership to Timothy. He commanded him to remind the flock of what lied ahead in order that they might live at a higher level: "Instruct them to do good, to be rich in good works, to be generous and ready to share, storing up for themselves the treasure of a good foundation for the future, so that they may take hold of that which is life indeed" (1 Timothy 6:18, 19). *Life indeed* refers to life with Jesus in eternity.

Unfortunately, many church leaders continue to teach that worldly goods can bring happiness. In a revealing *Time* magazine article entitled,

"Does God Want You to Be Rich?", David Van Buren and Jeff Chu present both sides in the debate over the prosperity gospel movement. On the "God wants us to be rich" side is Joel Osteen, pastor of Lakewood Church, a mega-church in Houston, Texas. The article states, "He and Victoria (Osteen's wife) meet with TIME in their pastoral suite, once the Houston Rocket's locker and shower area (the church meets in a former sports arena) but now a zone of overstuffed sofas and imposing oak bookcases. 'Does God want us to be rich?' he asks. 'When I hear the word rich, I think people might say, "Well, he's preaching that everybody's going to be a millionaire. I don't think that's it." Rather he explains, 'I preach that anybody can improve their lives. I think God wants us to be prosperous. I think he wants us to be happy. To me, you need money to pay your bills. I think God wants us to send our kids to college. I think he wants us to be a blessing to other people. But I don't think I'd say God wants us to be rich. It's all relative, isn't it?' The room's warm lamplight reflects softly off of his crocodile shoes."[48] The article also profiles one of Osteen's disciples: a man named George Adams who moved to Houston to be a part of Osteen's church. The "prosperity gospel" message is summed up in his quote, "Why not gain the whole world plus my soul?"[49] Unfortunately this unbiblical sentiment is shared by many other "Word of Faith" authors, ,preachers and teachers. Author and TV preacher Joyce Meyer says, "Who would want something where you're miserable, broke and ugly and you have to muddle through until you get to heaven?"[50]

Modern-day martyrs and many Christians of all colors and races "muddle through" until they get to heaven because their Lord suffered too. Joyce Meyer and men like Joel Osteen put too much emphasis on a life that can last up to one hundred years. Eternity lasts for…well… eternity. Why would I desire this world's goods, anyway? Isn't Jesus sufficient?

Jesus stands far above any material things or feelings that our culture offers. We live in a plastic world that abounds in false trickery. Madison Avenue is winning the battle because they're selling, and we're buying. But it's not just the secular world that's being affected; the world's system is sneaking into churches. Believers want Christ *and* the world, but the truth is, we can't have both.

D. Massimiliano Lorenzini of Frontline Ministries bluntly puts it this
way: "People now approach the church as consumers, just like everything
else in life… Religious content is losing relevance as people more and
more desire to have their *felt needs* met. People now want a religion that
works, or that they can use to make them happy. So in order to get people
into the church, church leaders are willing to give them what they want.
The name for this movement in Christianity is the Church Growth
Movement… theology is fast becoming an *embarrassing encumbrance.*
The doctrine of the utter otherness, or holiness, of God has been replaced
by the idol of the moral self. God is slick and slack, happiness is the opposite of righteousness, sin is self-defeating behavior, morality is a trade-off
of private interests, worship is entertainment, and the church is a mall in
which the religious, their pockets filled with the coinage of need, do their
business."[51] This statement, although troubling, is true: solid, biblical theology is hard to find these days. Churches instead advertise themselves as
happy places that will love everyone. This is a good thing, but do we even
know where our churches stand about doctrines relating to God?

Millard J. Erickson, one of the finest theologians of our time, is also
concerned about this problem: "This disappearance of theology can be
seen in two realms: the actual life of evangelicals and evangelical ministry.
Evangelical piety has become very internalized, very privatized, a devel-
opment that reflects the broader psychology of our day. At one time
happiness was considered by evangelicals to be a by-product of right
behavior. Now happiness has become the main goal of concern and activity. This experience of feeling good has increasingly become the object of
much evangelical activity. This has enabled it to be very successful, for the
consumer mentality simply is not hospitable to the habits of reflection
and judgment required to frame and defend orthodox belief…the *psy-
chologizing* of life undercuts historic Christianity at three points: (1) it
assumes the perfectibility of human nature, contrary to the Christian
gospel; (2) it undermines the desire and capacity to think, thus making
theology impossible; (3) it severs interest in the outside world, sacrificing
culture for self. Not only the understanding of the nature of evangelical-
ism but the understanding of ministry has been corrupted by
modernization…the pastor is seen as the CEO of a corporation…one's

occupation has become a career, in which advancing to larger, more financially rewarding, and more prestigious positions is the goal. It (this new style of ministry) has produced a kind of sentimentality 'that wants to listen without judging, that has opinions but little interest in truth, that is sympathetic but has no passion for that which is right.'"[52]

Christians continue to visit broken cisterns in their vain attempt to quench their thirst. Sadly, a generation of believers is becoming convinced that the *world* and the *gospel* are one and the same, but this just isn't true. Lasting treasure is only found in one place: it's called heaven. We just won't find it here on earth.

The faithful believer will taste the fruit of God's treasure-house. It'll contain *all* of the physical and emotional blessings that we now lack. Each believer must ask himself, *am I willing to wait to obtain real treasure, or will I settle for less so I can have it now?*

You can begin the process of motivating yourself to live a more meaningful Christian life by answering the following questions:

A. Are there longings deep in my soul that aren't being met? These could be longings for significance, appreciation, respect, intimacy with my spouse, or relationship.
B. What am I doing with these longings? Do I avoid them and pretend that they aren't there? Do I try to fill these longings with inappropriate demands on people, buying new things, or sinful behavior? Do I take them to the Lord and allow Him to satisfy my heart?
C. Am I convinced that decisions made in this life will impact eternity? Why or why not?
D. Am I afraid to desire eternal treasure because it seems selfish? What does the Bible teach on this matter?
E. What steps can I take to begin to accumulate eternal treasure? These steps may include a deeper prayer life, a new commitment to study the Bible, a new passion to love the people in my life and others, and becoming a vibrant part of a Christian community (church).
F. When the rubber meets the road, which is more important in my life: the world or the things of Christ? When I honestly answer this question, my life can change, and I can go to a higher level with Jesus.

Notes:

_____

_____

_____

_____

_____

_____

_____

_____

5. *I see the generosity, love, and glory of God.*
Eternal rewards reveal the character of God. He not only devised a plan to save us, but He's going to allow us to spend eternity with Him. For those who are faithful to Him, He will distribute crowns to them, and they will reign with Him as co-regents. As if that weren't enough, He desires eternal intimacy with us. He'll do all of this for a sinful race that rebelled against Him.

The apostle Paul was acutely aware of this majestic love. He expressed his gratitude to God in a letter written to a close associate named Titus: "But when the kindness of God our Savior and His love for mankind appeared, He saved us, not on the basis of deeds which we have done in righteousness, but according to His mercy, by the washing of regeneration and renewing by the Holy Spirit, whom He poured out upon us richly through Jesus Christ our Savior, so that being justified by His grace we would be made heirs according to the hope of eternal life" (Titus 3:4-7). This wonderful passage contains key words that give us the impression that Paul was absolutely captured by God's love. Words like "kindness," "saved," "mercy," "washing," "regeneration," "renewing," "poured," and "richly" show Paul's love and appreciation for all that God has done.

The apostle even calls us "heirs according to the hope of eternal life." This is Webster's definition of an heir: "1) one who inherits or is entitled to inherit property; 2) one who inherits or is entitled to succeed to a hereditary rank, title, or office (as in heir to the throne; and 3) one who receives or is entitled to receive some endowment or quality from a parent or predecessor." The Greek definition is simply "the one who gets the inheritance."

We'll inherit property when we reign over geographic locations. We'll receive a new title (*metochoi*), which means a "partner" with Jesus. Our parent (God) will give us these things because He loves us and is generous toward us: there's no other reason for this gift.

Every person who accepts Jesus as his personal Savior will be in heaven. Even though each believer will be an heir at some level, the Bible is clear that more will be given to the children who are the most faithful. In his letter to the Romans, where Paul laid out most of his theology, he writes, "The Spirit Himself testifies with our spirit that we are children of God, and if children, heirs also, heirs of God and fellow heirs with Christ, if indeed we suffer with Him so that we may also be glorified with Him. For I consider that the sufferings of this present time are not worthy to be compared with the glory that is to be revealed to us" (Romans 8:16-18).

Notice Paul's wording. He reminds us that it's the indwelling of the Holy Spirit that seals our salvation, but His children must "suffer with Him" in order to be "glorified with Him." Again, suffering and glorification are paired together. If I'm not willing to suffer for Christ, then I won't be glorified with Him; I won't be able to reign with Him. A listless Christian life will lead to less treasure. More important, a less than passionate believer will miss out on the full generosity of God.

John MacArthur writes, "Because he was created in the image of God, man was made with a glorious nature. Before the Fall, he was without sin and, in a way that Scripture does not reveal, he radiated the glory of his Creator. But when Adam fell by disobeying the single command of God, man lost not only his sinlessness and innocence but also his glory and its attendant dignity and honor. It's for that reason that all men now 'fall short of the glory of God' (Rom. 3:23). Fallen men seem basically to know they are devoid of glory and they often strive tirelessly to gain glory for themselves. The contemporary obsession with achieving self-esteem is a tragic reflection of man's sinful and futile efforts to regain glory apart from holiness. The ultimate purpose of salvation is to forgive and to cleanse men of their sin and to restore to them God's glory and thereby bring to Him still greater glory through the working of that sovereign act of grace. The glory that believers are destined to receive through Jesus Christ, however, will far surpass the glory man had before the Fall, because perfection far exceeds innocence. Glorification marks the completion and perfection of salvation."[53]

The struggle to obtain significance from this world doesn't stop with non-believers: Christians wrestle with this issue too. God's generosity and love are there for all to see, but we continually struggle to take hold of it. In a real sense, we fight an inner war. When we win spiritual battles, however, we get a glimpse of God's love and care for us.

In order to gain eternal treasure, we must be willing to fight. Oswald Chambers describes this severe inner struggle that should be taking place inside of every faithful believer: "It is only when God has transformed our nature and we have entered into the experience of sanctification that the fight begins. The warfare is not against sin; we can never fight against sin—Jesus Christ conquered that in His redemption of us. The conflict is waged over turning our natural life into a spiritual life. This is never done easily, nor does God intend that it be so. It's accomplished only through a series of moral choices. God does not make us holy in the sense that He makes our character holy. He makes us holy in the sense that He has made us innocent before Him. And then we have to turn that innocence into holy character through the moral choices we make. These choices are continually opposed and hostile to the things of our natural life which have become so deeply entrenched—the very things that raise themselves up as fortified barriers 'against the knowledge of God.' We can either turn back, making ourselves of no value to the kingdom of God, or we can determinedly demolish these things, allowing Jesus to bring another son to glory."[54]

The choice is ours. We'll see all of the Lord's generosity if we fight the battle. If we give up, we'll miss out on a myriad of eternal treasures, along with intimacy with Christ that comes when we reign with Him, the authority that comes with kingship, and a crown of glory. All of these things are made possible by the generosity and grace of God.

Rewards reveal the glory of God. We don't deserve to be saved, and we haven't earned the right to gain eternal treasure. We're far below God, but He's come down to our level. We tend to overlook eternal rewards because we don't appreciate their value since our culture has devalued the giver, who is God. The Bible speaks in clear terms about His majesty: "For as the heavens are higher than the earth, so are My ways higher than your ways and My thoughts than your thoughts" (Isaiah 55:9). Solomon said, "But will God indeed dwell with mankind on the earth? Behold heaven and the highest heaven cannot contain You…" (2 Chronicles 6:18a). After God miraculously opened the Red Sea and rescued Israel from the Egyptians, His people were appreciative of this divine feat: "Then Moses and the sons of Israel sang this song to the LORD, and said, 'I will sing to the LORD, for He is highly exalted…'" (Exodus 15:1). In Psalm 19, David was also captivated by God's glory: "The heavens are telling of the glory of God; and their expanse is declaring the work of His hands" (Psalm 19:1).

Scripture shouts about the glory and majesty of God. The sense of His glory is heightened when we understand that He made the decision to have a relationship with us. David couldn't get his mind around this amazing truth: "When I consider Your heavens, the work of Your fingers, the moon and the stars, which You have ordained; what is man that You take thought of him, and the son of man that You care for him? Yet You have made him a little lower than God, and You crown him with glory and majesty!" (Psalms 8:3-5). God is glorified by His mercy and kindness; He's exalted because He reached down to have intimacy with a lower and sinful race. How much more do we see His greatness when we realize He offers eternal rewards?

—

Mike Piazza was born in Norristown, Pennsylvania, in 1968. After playing high school baseball, Mike was still a long way from the major leagues. He was drafted in the 62nd round in the 1988 amateur draft, a round in which some teams have stopped drafting anyone. In fact, he was the 1,390th player overall to be drafted that year. He was signed by the Los Angeles Dodgers as a favor to his uncle: long-time manager Tommy Lasorda.

Piazza beat the odds and worked his way into the major leagues, becoming the rookie of the year in 1993. He signed a ground-breaking seven-year, ninety-one million dollar contract with the New York Mets in 1999 and led his team to the World Series. He has been an All-Star Game MVP and has slugged over four hundred home runs in his career. Mike Piazza has made it to the top, and he's certainly earned his rewards.

Mike's story can help us understand the richness and beauty of God within His gift of eternal rewards. Let's say that after the draft day in 1988, no team signed Mike Piazza, which wouldn't be unusual. Rarely do players who are drafted in these lower depths get beyond rookie-league or Class-A ball, even if they are signed. Assume that Piazza languished in the minors for five years before giving up and becoming a mechanic. Mike would have ended up doing nothing to earn anything from the baseball community. In fact, when he was drafted, baseball team owners had found 1,389 players who were better than he was.

One day, Mike's phone rings. It's the commissioner of baseball, who offers Mike a chance to attend any game with him for the rest of his life in the commissioner's box. Mike is surprised, but then agrees to attend a Dodgers game that night. Much to his astonishment, Mike is treated like royalty. He arrives at the ballpark and receives a private parking space. After filing through the ticket line, he is given an honorary lifetime pass to the stadium. Once inside, he's ushered to a private row of seats just above the visitor's dug-out. He is greeted with a warm handshake from the baseball commissioner, and the two begin a long-time friendship. Mike has been given the privilege of watching a baseball game every night with the commissioner; he didn't earn this.

A few weeks into the season, the commissioner informs Mike that he had just designated him to be in charge of the National League. Mike would be at his side while he traveled to the league's ballparks. Now, Mike had to say something. This was preposterous.

"Mr. Commissioner," Mike began. "I've enjoyed our time together and I count it a wonderful privilege to be your personal friend. I enjoy your company as we sit here and watch all of these games together.

Thank you for allowing me to run the National League. That showed a lot of faith in me. I appreciate that too. But I have to ask you one question."

"What's that, Mike?" the Commissioner wondered.

"Why? Why have you done all of this? I was a wash-out in baseball. I was one of the last guys drafted, and I only played for five years. There are many others who have gone to the Hall of Fame or have been the player of the year. Why did you choose me?" Mike stopped and waited. The commissioner paused for a moment, and a big grin spread across his face. He turned toward the former player.

"Mike, do you remember when you were playing for that Class-A team? It was a terrible team. The manager wasn't kind. Even though no one came to watch the games, you worked hard and did the very best with the talent you were given. That's why you're here. You took what was a little and honored me with your service. Now, I enjoy being around a man like that."

In real life, Mike Piazza is possibly the greatest catcher that has ever played the game. He may be a manager or work for the commissioner someday. If he does, it will be because of what he did for baseball.

In our story, the fictional Mike did nothing for baseball but was rewarded because of the generosity of the commissioner. He honored a faithful servant, not because he had to, but because he wanted to. That's true generosity and grace.

There are no perfect analogies to try and understand God's grace regarding eternal rewards. However, if you picture yourself sitting next to the commissioner of baseball, the President, or Bill Gates at a board meeting, the reality may begin to set in. We can rule with someone far greater and more wonderful than any of these men. We can reign with Christ—not because we deserve it, but because of His love and care for us.

He will look at the faithful believer one day and say something like, "Well done, my faithful one. I can't wait to spend time with you. I've been looking forward to this for a long time. You're precious to me. Wait until you see the rewards I have waiting for you. I know you're going to like them because I made them just for you. When I was on the Cross, I was thinking of you and pictured this day in My mind. Looking forward to this made it all worthwhile. You and I would reign together, and your throne would be next to mine. I'm glad you chose Me, even when it was hard. Satan was a very powerful enemy. There were times when you forgot about Me. I grieved during those times because I wanted this day to be special. But you persevered, and now we'll have many hours and days to talk. I created you, and I enjoy you. This is a wonderful day. You'll like your crown. It's beautiful; I know because I made it. Wear it with joy. Every time I look at you, I'll have joy. I'll remember that I was more important to you than things of the world. I will watch you wear your crown and beam with pride. I'm so glad you're here!"

An undeserved salvation by grace alone allows us to be saved. Faithfulness during our Christian life gives us a key to a storehouse of eternal treasure. Each key is provided by God; the only reason He has done this is because He loves us. His love is unreachable, unfathomable, and indescribable, but it can only be seen through eternal rewards. Each crown, jewel, and throne will reflect His character. Understanding this truth will cause you to give Him the glory that is due Him.

You can begin to accept God's love for you and understand His glory when you do the following:

A. Make a list of prayer requests and mark them off when they are answered. This will help you see the literal nature of God's grace.
B. Make a list of "God Moments"—times when God has moved in your life. These are events for which there is no other explanation other than the grace and generosity of God.
C. Make a mental note every time you see the sun, stars, moon, and the earth's beautiful scenery. This will help you exalt God as the creator of the universe. You will begin to get a sense of His transcendence over mankind and the longsuffering grace it took for Him to relate to us.
D. Make time during every prayer to thank God for His attributes, including His love, grace, compassion, and the fact that He is eternal, loving, unchanging, etc.
E. Make time to meditate on the reality of eternal rewards.

Notes:

_____

_____

_____

_____

_____

_____

_____

Eternal rewards can be yours in abundance, but please, don't take my word for it. I'm just an author. In order to gain eternal rewards:

1. *Commit yourself to prayer.* God will always show you the truth.
2. *Study the Bible.* Use good study tools. Take the time you need to find out the truth about where you stand with God and the reality of eternal rewards.
3. *Get involved with other Christians.* Be vulnerable. Fellowship will pave the way for accountability. You will be able to watch others and learn from them. You can also help them in return, using your own experiences.
4. *Sit under a solid Bible teacher.* Find a man who teaches the Word and applies it to daily life. Weigh his words with the words of the Bible. You need to eat solid spiritual food. Don't rely on the world to feed you.
5. *Read Christian authors that will challenge you to go deeper.* I have used quotes from many authors in this book. Read their books, or go to your local Christian bookstore and find books that will challenge you to focus on eternity. Stay away from books that focus only on the here and now.
6. *Listen to good Christian music.* Music was created by God to encourage us. When we listen to words about God, it helps us to focus on Him each day.

There are some excellent ways to earn eternal treasure, but these things will help you begin.

Remember, our journey to the throne will be a lifetime pilgrimage. There'll be good and bad times. Satan will attack you, and sacrifices will be required. The road will also be full of joy and wonder; we'll see God in a new and wonderful light because His blessings will be new each day. We'll be renewed in His presence as we learn to have intimacy with Him. The journey is long, but worthwhile. Your life will be maximized when you put your shoes on and run the race.

At the finish line, you will find trophies, rewards, thrones, territories, a partnership, a kingship, and more than you ever dreamed. Faithfulness is the key. Be faithful in all you do, and you will "trade up." I leave you with the words of Luke: "He who is faithful in a very little thing is faithful also in much; and he who is unrighteous in a very little thing is unrighteous also in much. Therefore if you have not been faithful in the use of unrighteous wealth, who will entrust the true riches to you? And if you have not been faithful in the use of that which is another's, who will give you that which is your own?'" (Luke 16:10-12).

---

28. Chitwood, Judgment Seat of Christ, 1.
29. Zane C. Hodges, The Gospel Under Siege; A Study on Faith and Works (Dallas: Redencion Viva, 1982), 10.
30. Dwight J. Pentecost, Things to Come; A Study in Biblical Eschatology. (Findlay: Durham, 1958), 220.
31. Paul Helm, The Last Things: Death, Judgment, Heaven, Hell. (Edinburgh: Banner of Truth and Trust, 1989), 62.
32. Edward Hickman, ed., The Works of Jonathan Edwards: Volume One. (Edinburgh: Banner of Truth and Trust, 1834), 656.
33. E. Schuyler English, "The Church At the Tribunal," in Prophetic Truth Unfolding Today, Charles Lee Feinberg, ed. (Old Tappan: Fleming H. Revell Co., 1968), 29.
34. Dillow, The Reign of the Servant Kings, 561.
35. Quick, Living for the Kingdom, 164-165.
36. Robert H. Mounce, The Book of Revelation: The New International Commentary on the New Testament (Grand Rapids: Eerdmans, 1977), 104.

37. Quick, Living for the Kingdom, 174-175.
38. Quick, Living for the Kingdom, 233-234.
49. Mounce, The Book of Revelation, 135.
40. Dillow, The Reign of the Servant Kings, 564.
41. Dillow, The Reign of the Servant Kings, 548.
42. Walvoord and Zuck, Bible Knowledge Commentary, 795.
43. "Before the Next Sex Scandal", Christianity Today Editorial, April 1, 2006, www.ctilibrary.com. © Used by permission, "Christianity Today", 2006.
44. "Before the Next Sex Scandal", 2006.
45. Richard A. Murphy, Maranatha Life.P.O. Box 1206, Donna, TX 78537, 2002, www.maranathalife.com.
46. Grudem, Systematic Theology, 1161.
47. Robert Lewis, Men's Fraternity, The Great Adventure (Little Rock: Fellowship Bible Church and Fellowship Associates, Inc., 2006), p.16.
48. Jeff Chu and David Van Biema, "Does God Want Us To Be Rich?", Time Magazine, September, 2006. www.time.com,
49. Jeff Chu and David Van Biema, "Does God Want Us To Be Rich?"
50. Jeff Chu and David Van Biema, "Does God Want Us To Be Rich?"
51. D. Massimiliano Lorenzini, "Current Challenges to the Church", Front Line Ministries, copyright © 2002-2006, www.frontlinemin.org
52. Millard J. Erickson, Postmodernizing the Faith: Evangelical Responses to the Challenge of Postmodernism (Grand Rapids: Baker Books, 1998), 34-35.
53. John MacArthur, MacArthur's New Testament Commentary: Romans 1-8.,Electronic Edition STEP Files,1997, Parsons Technology, Inc., PO Box 100, Hiawatha, Iowa.
54. Oswald Chambers. My Utmost for His Highest (Uhrichsville, OH: Barbour Publishing Inc., 1935-c1992), 252.

Epilogue

The Lord's voice resonated like thunder, deep and authoritative. Yet, the tone contained warmth and reminded me of a teacher I had in school. On the outside, he seemed stern and unyielding, but on the inside, he had a great love for his students.

I knew that whatever words I heard would stick for eternity: there would be no going back. Whatever Jesus was about to say, His words would stand forever. Second chances were over, and "another try" meant nothing. This was it—my judgment at the *bema*. I knelt and waited.

"My son," Jesus began. He gave me the warmest smile I had ever seen. His arms beckoned me forward. "Please come here."

"Yes, Lord." The security guard walked over and helped me to my feet.

"Do you know where you are?" He asked.

"I think so. Is this the judgment?"

"Yes," He replied. "It's your judgment. We are going to look at your life. First, I want to say that I am glad you are My son. I am thrilled that you accepted Me as your Savior. I want you to know that you will be in heaven for all of eternity."

"Thank you, Jesus," is all I could manage.

"Now, let's look at your life. Your motives and actions are going to determine your place in My kingdom. Do you understand?"

"Yes."

"Good. Let's get started."

A strange sensation came over me. I became engrossed in my earthly life as I was reliving it. I clearly saw the good decisions I had made and felt great joy. There was also a clear account of times when I had put God aside. For these times, I felt a sense of loss and shame.

I couldn't believe how many times I had chosen the world over Jesus. These decisions seemed reasonable at the time, but now, I realized they were foolish. I looked at Jesus, and He looked at me. I didn't know that I loved Him this much. I felt a deep sadness that I had chosen not to pursue Him at certain times and disappointed Him. My life was now clearly shown; everything was in the open. Parts of it disgusted me, while others gave me joy. It was the Lord's turn to speak again.

"I've been looking forward to our time together," He said. "It'll now be my joy to reward you for your faithfulness." He was proud of me and applauded me. The Lord told me about how much He loved me and appreciated my service.

"Here is your crown." It was breathtaking and more beautiful than anything I'd ever seen, its jewels glistening in the light of His presence. He continued, "You will have a throne on which to reign." He showed me the territory for which I'd be responsible. "Well done. You will reign with me."

My judgment was over. I wasn't going to reign over the largest piece of land, and my crown didn't have as many jewels as some others. For that, I was sorry. If I could take back certain decisions that I made on earth, I would, but it was too late. I was offered many chances to enlarge God's kingdom on earth. There were times when I rose to the occasion, but there were many times that I failed. I understood that now and for all of eternity. It caused me great sadness, but it also caused me to more deeply understand God's grace. I was here! I was standing in the presence of Christ because of His grace. I was starting a new life, reigning with Christ! *Well done*, He had said.

Joy rushed through me. I felt important. Eternity was going to be good—very good.

A Note to the Unsure

You may not be sure if you're a Christian. I'll take you through some brief steps that will help you begin a new relationship with Christ. Then, you can "trade up" and have access to these marvelous eternal rewards.

The Gospel message is easy to understand:

1. *All of us have sinned and made poor decisions.* The Bible says: "All have sinned and come short of the glory of God" (Romans 3:23). You must understand that you're a sinner.
2. *The penalty for these poor choices is eternal separation from God in hell:* "For the wages of sin is death…" (Romans 6:23). You and I are on the way to hell without the grace of Jesus. Someone must pay the price for sin, and this is what Jesus did. We must accept the fact that we can be saved from the penalty that awaits us. Now comes the good news:
3. *God sent Jesus into the world to die on the cross to save you and me:* "For God so loved the world, that He gave His only begotten Son, that whoever believes in Him shall not perish, but have eternal life" (John 3:16).
4. *God is pursuing you.* He loves you and wants you to be His child. He desires that you reign with Him throughout all eternity. He may be

knocking on the door of your heart right now: "Behold, I stand at the door and knock; if anyone hears My voice and opens the door, I will come in to him and will dine with him, and he with Me" (Revelation 3:20).

If you feel the pull of God and understand that you need Jesus, now is the time to make a decision to follow Him for the rest of your life. All you need to do is ask and He'll save you. If you've never prayed or are unsure of what to say, you can use this prayer model. Say it in your own words and mean it. A new life is waiting for you!

Prayer for Salvation:

Father God, I know that I've made poor choices. I know that I'm a sinner. I believe that your Son, Jesus, came to save me. I believe that He died on the cross and paid the penalty for my sin. Please forgive me for my sin and throw it away. I believe that the Holy Spirit will now come into my heart. I believe that I will be your child for all of eternity. Thank you for saving me. Amen.

You're now a Christian! Don't do anything until you tell someone. Write down the time and date on this book or in your Bible so you will always be reminded that this decision was real. Find a church in the phone book or on-line. It's time for you to "trade up!"